Table of contents:

Preface

"Freedom is never more than one generation away from extinction."

— Ronald Reagan

This document will provide a framework for understanding the ideology of the Fourth Way. I will attempt throughout this document to provide a true middle path to politics which will aim to play on the basic and simplistic values of human evolution and thought and combat the failing traditional ideologies of the modern left and right whose idiosyncratic ideas are creating more problems than they are solving, and are bringing about the collapse of the greatest civilisation and achievements of man. The political ideology that is represented throughout this book is that of civilisational libertarianism.

Consistency and Understanding

1. Firstly, when I reference throughout this document "civilisation" what I am referring to is the different societies throughout history whose cultures have been pre-established, dominant in their

respective hemispheres and under whom a great number of peoples are united as one. Historically, these examples include the ancient Roman Republic and Empire and Ancient China. When attempting to assess whether a society is a civilisation or a culture, one can look at that particular nation in depth. For example, in the case of ancient Greece, it is illogical to describe the Greek states as being one. Yes, they may have shared the same culture, but they were not a united state and suffered from constant infighting, and this continued well into the conquest of Alexander III who did unite the Greeks but faced tumultuous amounts of opposition during his reign from the likes of Sparta, Athens and Corinth. Another example of a culture and not a civilisation can be seen in the Empire of Great Britain. Even though Great Britain dominated several hemispheres, their culture was not dominant over the people it ruled. The British Raj stayed uniquely Indian. This can indeed be seen commonly with cultural nations rather than civilisations as foreign cultures can easily rub off onto dominant cultures. A great example of this is the British Raj, I would go as far as to argue that the British Empire was actually more of an Anglo-Indian empire with Indias huge culture rubbing off onto the British way of life and its culture being extraordinarily well maintained during the Empire. A similar case can be seen with Macedon under Alexander III. Despite the fact that Macedon grew to conquer half of the known world at this time, the reality is that the Macedonian elite began to accept Persian ideals, with Alexander believing himself to be a God by his death, a very unkingly attribute within Macedon, but an idea that within Persia was not only normal but expected of a king. Now we will look at an example of a civilisation. America was founded from the decaying corpse of British intellectual thought. America today, despite the turbulence of its political system is a dominant nation on the world stage and is relatively united. Most Americans do want what is best for the American Empire, even if those views contradict each other at times. This is the flow of human cooperation on a historical level. America dominates its hemisphere, and its culture is one of socialism, based around practical individualism and a mindset of doing what is best for the group, even sacrificing idealism and one's individuality to get to this point. This is a true civilisation of colossal magnitude.

2. Social Intuitionism refers to Jonathan Haidt's work on moral psychology and its principles. Haidt established a new model of psychology and

thought in his work "The Righteous Mind", which actively determines how people respond to different moral questions and pursuits based on their score in different categories. These scores then often show a pattern of correlation to an individual's political beliefs and moral beliefs.

3. Despite personal beliefs, throughout this reflection all references to a divine authority of any kind will be named "Providence" and not God. The intention of this reflection is not to provide religious beliefs or new theology but to rebuild political philosophy from its foundations and build a new reality. Religion in this book is of

no concern, unless discussing public morals.

4. This reflection will talk extensively about "truth". In this sense, this means reality and its realities. What we know to be true can only be proved practically and through empirical evidence. Statistics will not necessarily prove a truth as a left-winger might espouse, as many statistics taken by intellectuals are nearly impossible to actually be taken seriously. I remember once reading a sociology book that stated sociologist investigated citizen's attitude to work who were dependent on benefits and came to the conclusion their attitudes are no different to the upper classes

attitudes to work, yet when looked at realistically, what kind of a person would openly admit they are lazy in an investigation on stereotypes against the poor? It would be idiotic and distasteful to attempt to purposely depict your own laziness as a reality when it is negative and re-asserts stereotypes against your person which you don't like. Another issue with statistics is that they are often snippets in time and do not properly reflect the nature of changing landscapes. We will look at this idea more later on in this reflection when discussing the economy and intellectualism.

Introduction

"The truth is not for all men, but only for those who seek it."
— Ayn Rand

This reflection will provide a reality of what it means to be a true centrist.

As a starting point, it is important to address all key principles that will make up this book. First is truth without lies. There can be absolutely no room for lies in society any longer. We must accept realities as they are and accept that there is a natural aspect to life that cannot be changed regardless of personal views on liberty and freedom or even desire. A most dangerous and chaotic untruth has spread in our modern world, the idea that an untruth can become a truth, and thus all untruths are a viable possibility to be made into truth by whatever professional or intellectual first opens their mouths. A key example of this can be seen in the transgender movement. I will start by saying I am not transphobic, and later in this book you will see that I provide scientific evidence in support of transgender people to be able to live their lives how they please, but with that being said, the idea that a man born with XY chromosomes can become a full woman with XX chromosomes is preposterous. A trans-woman will maintain between 80%-90% of their muscle mass from prior to transitioning from being a man[1] and will still maintain at least a 12% larger strength advantage over a cisgender woman in all sporting activities.[2] This is a clear example where the need to pretend has indefinitely clouded the judgement of civilisations and has damaged truth. It is not a bad thing to want to seek equality for all, as we are going to see throughout this

---

[1]Wiik, A., Lundberg, T. R., Rullman, E., et al. (2020). *Muscle strength, size, and composition following 12 months of gender-affirming treatment in transgender individuals.* The Journal of Clinical Endocrinology & Metabolism, 105(3)

Roberts, T. A., Smalley, J., & Ahrendt, D. (2020). Effect of gender affirming hormones on athletic performance in transwomen and transmen: implications for sporting organisations and legislators. *British Journal of Sports Medicine*, **54**(11)

reflection which is Libertarian in nature, but we cannot afford to mask untruths with the guise of justice and pretend that this is equalitarian, as there cannot be true equality without truth. What I mean by this is simple, if a person born with XY chromosomes transitions into being a woman after suffering from gender dysphoria, they will still have a major advantage over women in sports, whose separate category was created to give women their own space for competition. Common arguments against this include ideas that “it is only a minority of trans-women that compete in sports”, and while this may be true, any exception of this kind that strays from truths is very dangerous and is not liberty, but a lie. Blurring the lines between truth and untruth is the direct link between degeneracy and a collapsing society as we will see later in this book. Truth must exist for all that is good to exist, so we should be chivalrous in our pursuit of it and not allow our opinions to cloud realities and lead us to untruths. This idea will become extremely important later in our discussions on economics.

The second most important foundational aspect to consider in this reflection is that of liberty without chaos. Every individual in our society should have the absolute and fundamental right to choose how to live their life in the pursuit of happiness. This principle provides the building blocks of this ideological approach, but it is not one-sided and must be respectful. We must wholeheartedly recognise that the only way to maintain our liberty is to rely on the state and its government to protect us from alien cultures with illiberal values and from tyrants from all parts of the world. The future of humanity will not be under the boot of a tyrant, which within itself is its own form of chaos, but through individuals and their right to choose. We also cannot allow ourselves to diverge into identity politics, which damages the prospect of the individual by collectivising one group of individuals against another. I of course accept that society must be egalitarian and filled with individuals who are free to make their own choices, and so when this is threatened it is the duty of the government and every individual to act to prevent the removing of liberty or the spread of untruths and to defend freedom. Chaos must also not be tolerated. I accept the right of any individual to do what they please with their own lives but we must not allow society to diverge into chaos and lawlessness. Some of my libertarian colleagues vehemently have argued that you should have the right to ask someone to end your own life. There have been many cases, particularly in the United States when sick individuals have asked another individual to murder them as some sort of sexual fantasy such as the German criminal case of Armin Meiwis. Meiwis posted a request on a forum to see if anyone wanted to be ate. Bernd Jürgen Brandes responded and the two met. Meiwis sauteed his penis and the two of them ate it. Meiwis then murdered Brandes and ate parts of his body.[3] A libertarian may suggest that this is acceptable as the two adults consented to this, but this is a perfect

---

[3]Stampf, G. & Brown, P., 2008. *Interview with a Cannibal: The Secret Life of the Monster of Rotenburg*. Los Angeles: Phoenix Books.

example of chaos taking hold of human life through belief in liberty. This is not true liberty as it killed a man, even if consensual. I widely accept John Stuart Mills ideological approach to the harm principle, but for those within my own nation. I would not hesitate to destroy any foreign threat which may endanger the liberty of my citizens or their safety and the safety of our children. Thus, liberty must exist without chaos and there must be a balance of free choice and anti-primitivism.

Third, we must accept that order must exist without tyranny. The most easy way to create order is to build an egotistically individualist society. This can be seen with the founding of the United States. Thomas Jefferson originally foresaw a state of complete agrarian freedom, a loose confederation of individuals and their delegates in a decentralised confederate legislature. However, what actually occurred in the United States due to freedom of opportunity was a situation in which families and men competed in their own vicinities or states for the best jobs, the best business partners, and the best education for their children. This pursuit of wealth and fulfilment over the European nations which were primarily concerned with religious dogma, maintenance of a feudal hierarchy and mass imperialistic expansionism, created an American society where the success of one individual would in turn lead to the success of other individuals through opportunity of employment and business partnership, which in turn created a society of order and business. [4] Of course there must be limits to personal will. I deliberately say "will" here and not "freedom" because is having the ability (or right) to hurt someone "freedom"? I think not, it appears to me to be deviance. Without these limits to personal will, the liberties of other will be hurt and chaos will consume society, as revenge and the need for revenge spread like wildfire. Thus, order has to exist for a stable society, but we cannot allow order and the fear of loss of control to spiral into tyranny. After nine-eleven and the Iraq War began, Vice-President of the United States Richard "Dick" Cheney took control of the White House and effectively ruled as a shadow

---

[4]de Riencourt, A. (1957). *The Coming Caesars, p. 282*. New York: Coward-McCann.

president who held massive sway over the president. It was Cheney's political patronage that built Bush's cabinet. Donald Rumsfeld, Cheney's mentor since the Ford administration and long-time ally was made the secretary of defence, David Addington the White House legal counsel was effectively owned by Cheney and used to dominate legal structures across the country to justify the introduction of the torture of prisoners of war and those suspected of terrorist sympathies, Scooter Libby the assistant to the president of national security affairs was totally loyal to the vice-president and operated as his right hand man within the administration. Cheney's influence allowed him to bypass the President's secretary of State Collin Powell and circumvent the entire state department to justify his war on Iraq. This is a perfect example of a democracy spiralling into shadow government tyranny, or at the very least a fear of chaos driving tyrannical actions. Cheney saw the worst in all nations and believed in the future that Iraq would work with terrorist states to destroy the United States, and so he enacted sweeping measures to restrict personal freedom and destroy rights like privacy and fair trial.[5]

Lastly, religion should exist but without dogma. Fundamentalism and dogmatic tradition are a threat to liberty and the evolution of humanity. I will not be delving deeply into religion throughout this book, but I will be explaining here that dogmatic belief is terrible for a civilisation as it stagnates

---

[5]Gellman, B. (2008). *Angler: The Cheney Vice Presidency*. Penguin Press.

its discoveries and pushes it into the past. This can be entirely seen in the rise and decline of the Islamic world during the early modern period. The Islamic civilisation was the most advanced on the planet prior to the early modern period, only being rivalled by China. However, by the rise of the early modern period largely due to radical Sunni Imams and their role in governance of the Islamic world, Madrasas moved away from teaching philosophy and science towards teaching theology, while a strict adherence code to the Koran was developed away from rational interpretation. This severely limited the intellectual capability of the Islamic world which began to decline massively by the 1700s and began to collapse. During the Islamic Golden Age, 12% of books were written on scientific topics but by 1700 that number was just 2%.[6]

So, to summarise, throughout this brief introduction we have laid the foundations of this political philosophy. Truth takes primacy and sovereignty above everyone including individual liberty, partly because, without truth there cannot be liberty. It is the same philosophical problem as direct realism versus indirect realism. If we sense everything directly and perceive what we see to be true then we can build liberty based on rational thought of what we know to be true. However, the problem is that our sense of reality may be miscalculated due to a series of

---

[6]Edis, T. (2007). *An Illusion of Harmony: Science and Religion in Islam*. Amherst, NY: Prometheus Books.

misrepresentations and distortions of reality. If a person saw a pink elephant and never saw another elephant for the rest of their life, they would likely believe that elephants were pink upon their death, not realising their grasp of reality has been twisted likely by the pink paint on the elephant that they saw. This is the same problem of living a life of true liberty through truth. You cannot have liberty without truth as our sense of reality may be directly altered by misrepresentations and thus giving us a false sense of liberty that isn't real. An example of this can be seen in government propaganda or cover ups. Truth is incredibly important as it gives us as clear as a direct grasp of reality as possible, allowing us to live and individual life grounded in liberty which is grounded in truth. Liberty must exist without animalistic tendency, order must persist in social structure to prevent the rise of chaos and tyranny, and religion can exist without dogma and its creations of extremist ideology.

THE CHIVALROUS
ALWAYS FIGHT
FOR TRUTH

God is Evolution

"Evolution is not a force but a process. Not a cause but a law."

— John Morley

God as we understand divine providence is evolution. Throughout this chapter I will attempt to highlight this belief as accurately as possible and explain the beliefs behind it.

The universe has so many rules when we look closely enough but we never seem to pay attention to them. One of these rules is what I will call "divine extinction". Whenever a disease becomes too good at spreading itself to new hosts and evolves to a point of becoming immune to antidote, it destroys all its hosts causing itself to die out. When the outlook of a civilisation becomes too good, and conditions are too well off for its people, those people delve into degeneracy and become lazy, causing the civilisation to collapse. A perfect example of this in practice can be seen in the "rat utopia experiment", also known as the "Universe 25" experiment when rats were given an unlimited supply of food, shelter and water. The experiment was designed to see the effects of resource abundance and dense population on animal behaviour. A small group of rats was first introduced, who bred very quickly producing massive amounts of offspring. Very quickly, as these offspring matured, new behaviours were observed. The main effect of the experiment was that the male rats started to exhibit more feminine behaviours. Established hierarchies quickly began to break down, with there being a small group of dominant male rats and very large groups of feminine male rats. Homosexual behaviour was observed among both male and female rats. Female rats in particular became unusually aggressive and stopped nurturing their young, causing infant mortality rates to collapse. In the final phase of the experiment, deviant sexual behaviours were observed more frequently as well as a massive reduction in the birth rate and excessive grooming among both male and female rats, who were labelled "the beautiful ones". By the end of the colony, male and female rats could no longer form normal social bonds because they lacked parental models and so reproduction halted entirely causing the colony to die out, despite having unlimited food and water.[7] The effects of this experiment can be seen in every civilisation and even in the modern world today. After the second world war, resources became much more abundant due to an increasingly open and globalised economy as well as rapid economic growth, as factories previously geared towards production of military equipment now began manufacturing civilian items. Very quickly a rapid growth in population occurred, which we now recognise as "the baby boom" of the 1950s. In the modern day now, most recognise that there is some sort of crisis

---

[7]Calhoun, J. B. (1962). *Population density and social pathology*. **Scientific American**, 206(2), 139–148.

of masculinity. Homosexual behaviour has steadily increased through every generation since the baby boom. According to a Gallup poll, traditionalist seniors (those born prior to 1946) are only 0.8% self-identifying gay, this then rises slowly to 2.6% among boomers, then 4.2% among generation X, 11% among Millennials and 19.5% among members of generation Z.[8] Following this trend, regardless of argumentation of transparency increasing in more recent times, there is a very clear and apparent increase in homosexual lifestyles, particularly increasing from the boomer generation. So, it is becoming increasingly clear that social norms which were previously considered degenerate are increasingly becoming

---

[8]**Jones, J. M.** (2022). *LGBT Identification in U.S. Ticks Up to 7.1%.*

normal, as life continues to increase in quality. I want to say quickly, that even despite this truth, we must find a way to allow people to live how they like. We must build society from the ground up and ensure that liberty is maximised but also sustainable and we will investigate ways this can be achieved through education and the family structure, regardless of what gender the parents are.

I want to point out immediately that I am not being transphobic or homophobic later on this reflection I will provide scientific and evolutionary evidence to support both ways of life. I am also not personally heterosexual. But, following the reality of truths and untruths, this is something that needs to be recognised and discussed. Continuing forward, another rule of the universe is hierarchy. No matter what society is established there is and always will be a hierarchy. Putting aside the Soviet Union for a second, any other attempt at the building of a truly Marxian socialist nation would still have a hierarchy. There would be intellectuals who would study and espouse the words of Marx and who the people would look up to. There would be workers on the factory committee who would undoubtedly be more gifted in oratory rhetoric and so would be able to sway the rest of the workers one way or another on work issues. Though it could be argued that these circumstances are minimal, the reality is where to draw the line? How long until that influential factory worker is practically considered the boss of the workers because he holds so much influence over them? This may sound like a simple argument but there are people who would actually argue that true equality can exist in a Marxian state and a utopia can be made, when the reality is that this utopia cannot exist because its collapse is inevitable due to basic human nature.

This leads to the next rule of universe, that inequality will always exist. It is impossible for equality not to exist. This is where I will diverge for a second and highlight that there are two types of discrimination, man-made discrimination, and natural discrimination. You cannot consider the Jim Crow laws of the south to be a product of natural discrimination, rather it was enforced and created by man. Equally, you cannot consider a child born into a poor family to be a result of man-made discrimination, rather it is a result of natural discrimination, thus why is it fair that that man should try to make up for this unfortunate natural discrimination? Rawlsian modern liberals may try to argue that life can be equated to a game, where prior to the game you are allocated a spot on the board randomly, and thus if your spot was unfair, you would demand a change in the rules. While this is a true and likely aspect of the competitive nature of humanity, the reality is that it is human nature to seek better circumstance and so instead of trying to create massively inefficient welfare states in pursuit of democratic equality, the reality is that the poor must always exist and persevere to try to improve their own circumstances. Their success in turn will fuel the success of other poor people as the success of an individual, fuels the success of society as a whole. As well as this idea, the success of the upper classes does improve the success of the lower classes, but we will address this later in the economics section. I do recognise the need for limited positive discrimination in cases of academia. The reason I recognise this as an exception is simply because I am entirely a meritocrat and so it is important that the most intelligent in society rise to the pinnacle of the hierarchy, despite their wealth, connections and influence. Another incendiary statement I will make is that the Great Chain of Being not only exists but is essential to understanding the life of humanity and its journey through history. The Great Chain of Being as it existed during the medieval and early modern period is not accurate, but it can be seen as a first step towards understanding how sociological structures work. The aspect of the Great Chain of Being that our ancestors got wrong was the idea that it is somehow blood related. This is wrong, as blood means nothing. We are all distantly related to some sort of nobility or royalty and the essence of what it means to be human cannot be summed up based on the character of one's blood. Instead, the Great Chain of Being does exist but it is primarily concerned with one's education and knowledge. The best and brightest of society may have a head start in moving up the great chain, but the reality is that it is only one's expanded knowledge and retained knowledge that can make them more godlike. I must explain the hierarchy in its stages now starting from the bottom and working up:

1. The enslaved stage
2. The gentry intellectual stage
3. The enlightened stage
4. The chivalrous stage.

The purpose of this investigation is not to portray a set of pre-conceived notions by which one can rise up the Great Chain, but instead it will give a brief overview of what it means to be in either stage.

1. The enslaved stage: The common man, with a common job, with a common education. This man has no concern for reality or its meanings. He is a slave to his own fulfilment and joy through working a tireless job and living a tireless life. This

man cannot be considered anything more than a slave to his own pleasures. Examples of this stage may include tradesman, dock workers or receptionists.

2. The intellectual stage: This mean has an education ranging into the university degrees but cannot be considered enlightened as he is a social intellectual who follows what the enlightened tell him to do. He has very little real interest in books or learning more outside of his degree. This is where most people in the modern world are placed, examples of this category may include scientists and lecturers.

3. The enlightened stage: This man has a thirst for

knowledge that cannot be matched by a simple degree. He aims consistently not only for academic excellence but for research outside of his fields and grasping with an understanding of reality. This person doesn't just espouse the ideas of other enlightened but actively seeks to understand reality and critical concepts themselves examples of this category can include philosophers like Edmund Burke and Benjamin Disraeli.

4. The chivalrous stage: These are the types of men who have become the closest to what the medieval Chain of Being would consider as being "God". Instead of including religious aspects to the Chain of Being we

will instead consider those closest to the top as being "Godly". These are people who have an understanding of reality and themselves unfounded by any other person. These are the types of men and women which change history and are remembered for their actions and great works. Examples of this type of person may include Plato, Aristotle and Machiavelli.

It is important to note that I am not arguing for a set reality or set hierarchy. Meritocracy is not set in stone and the leaders of today must be ready for themselves or their children to be the ordinary citizens of tomorrow. In effect you can move down the Great Chain of Being throughout your life if you let your work ethic or intellectual rigour slip or stop contributing meaningfully to society. What I am instead arguing for is meritocracy based on survival of the fittest. A person may be born with an IQ of 140 but achieve very little in their lives as they are enslaved by pleasure, massively reducing their work ethic, which in turn contributes very little to society. In contrast, a person with an IQ of 90 may be born and have an amazing work ethic and go on to attend the top universities like Oxford and Princeton despite them being born with a disadvantage to the person with a lower IQ. In either case, it is the individual's actions and work ethic that will allow them to travel up the Great Chain of Being. I recognise that there is an unfair difference in born attributes in either case, but it is impossible for a government to constantly cater to individually circumstances as Rawls suggested. Should a government give money to a middle-class family because their child was born with a lower IQ than a child in a poor family with a relatively high IQ? This is of course entirely unfair and while critics may argue that the wealthier family already has the money to make their child do well in education, the reality of the matter is that government intervention to try to solve these types of perceived inequalities would be wholly ineffective and create a tyrannical interventionist government that would be a major burden on personal freedom. Measures taken by the government to try and even out these types of social dilemmas are ineffective as there are so many different variables that go into potential success besides a person living in a deprived area or having a higher IQ than other individuals. Ability is hugely hard to measure and is multi-faceted with hundreds of variables. It also raises questions of morality that do not need to be raised, instead we should let the social hierarchy balance itself out based on personal will and desire not based on government wealth redistribution and intervention. A person born with a higher IQ may have an advantage in pursuit of a goal, as they can learn and process information much quicker, but the idea that they will use this advantage at all times putting someone with a lower IQ at a disadvantage is a fallacy because work ethics and personality types vary greatly between different people, as does opportunity. Therefore, the government ability to try to provide better equality of opportunity to all people is dumbfounded as it is uncontrollable and is constantly changing, similar to the economy. It is best to let people regulate themselves and pursue their own goals.

Another rule of the universe and that God is evolution is grounded in a moral truth. All life must be weighed as being hugely valuable to the course and evolution of humanity. This is one of the rules where determining what is reality through the lens of truth is hugely important. I don't think anyone would deny that upon fertilisation, the cell is a separate entity to the mother. It would be idiotic to suggest therefore, that the cell in question cannot grow into a fully-fledged human as this is the same process by which we came into existence. I am writing this reflection right now as a human who was fertilised and was given the chance to grow and develop. Human life is extremely complex. A chicken will lay multiple eggs at once and will care for them all in hopes they survive. A human gives birth to a baby before it is even able to communicate or hold its head up by itself. This shows the complexity of human life within itself. The point I am making is that, if there is a chance for life to spring from a one-night stand or even a contraception accident, that chance should not be taken from that "individual in waiting". In this situation, I will coin this unborn cell an "individual in waiting". It is not yet capable of taking care of itself, but it definitely has the chance to grow into a true individual who will flourish and can positively contribute to the upward evolution of man. The only time were exceptions to this kind of rule can be made is when the life of an already existing fully fledged individual is under threat of death. Thus, continuing with an analysis of abortion, if a miscarriage is about to take place that may threaten the mother's life, then an abortion is necessary. In the case of a young girl becoming pregnant, if a doctor feels that the pregnancy will threaten the girl's life then an abortion should be allowed. But in the case of one-night stands or accidental pregnancies, this should not be the first choice. Equally, if a person can no longer live their life to its maximum potential as a flourishing individual that contributes positively society, the option of assisted suicide should not be taken from their personal rights. However, this should not be considered in the case of mental issues as these people still have the possibility to recover and become flourishing individuals in the future with enough guidance and support. Regardless of these theoretical discussions, all life must be considered valuable as a basis of the rule of truth without lies. It is okay to be personally liberal and believe strongly in equality but we cannot put individual freedom or perceived freedom above truth as there cannot be true freedom without truth as we explored earlier in this reflection. We must look past our own biases and use the truth that life is more important than personal desires.

Another rule of the universe is that every civilisation has a spine. This spine is the core of the civilisation and is its essence. Its spine is its view on law, civic morals, myth and culture. If the spine of the civilisation is in danger, how a creative elite react to that danger will determine whether the civilisation will survive, and its DNA grow more complex. If the spine is not saved and it becomes tainted, it will collapse and the civilisation or culture will die. There is no country on Earth that takes their constitution as seriously as the United States. It makes the basis for civic morality: you can carry a gun to defend yourself and have unlimited access to free speech; it makes the basis for law: there have been cases of legal prattle in the US of lawyers going as far as to analyse the word "person" from the US constitution to determine legal right; and to an extent its myth and contribution to America's culture can also be seen: the Founding Fathers have become legendary figures in United States history and are almost treated godlike by many Americans. An example of a spine collapsing can be seen in Weimar

Germany. The country had just been handed on embarrassing defeat at the hands of the allies in the Treaty of Versailles and the nation quickly became consumed with anarchy. The failed Socialist Spartacist rising in 1919 saw fighting on the streets. This led to the rise of the Frei Korp and the Kapp Putsch when Berlin was occupied by a right-wing military Junta who aimed to re-impose monarchy on Germany and rebuild its national identity, but was overthrown by the workers at the hands of the Weimar government. After years of chaos, Germany experienced 4 "Golden Years" under the steady hand of Gustav Stresemann but would soon find itself riddled with hopelessness once again when the Wall Street Crash sank the economy. Germany had received 25 billion dollars in American investments between 1924 and 1929 through the

Dawes plan (1924) and Young plan (1929). America recalled these international investments to attempt to boost liquidity in their own economy and this removed the bedrock of the German economy. It was then Hitler as an economic socialist and social ethnic nationalist who was able to gain control of the minds of the German people. His Socialist economics, though moderate, appealed greatly to the struggling German masses and even the business classes who were promised a safe business environment away from foreign competition. His ethnic nationalist stances appealed with German conservatives and patriots who were still wounded by the defeat of the First World War and sought retribution for their nation. Hitler attempted to embody the civilisational spine of Germany and his ploy worked, as he was made chancellor on the 30th January 1933, commanding the largest party in the Reichstag with 37% of seats. The destruction he unfolded on Germany with his destructive world war could've saw the collapse of German civilisation, but once again a new leader, Konrad Adaneur, would save Germany from the brink of destruction by rebuilding its economy and securing political stability. We can see here how a creative minority continuously aims to secure the civilisational spine of their nation to attempt to save it from destruction or turmoil, this is the natural course of history, and we will look at this in much greater detail in the next chapter.

The last major rule of God being evolution is that the universe constantly seeks equilibrium and tries to balance its natural forces to seek a constant state of being, just as a radioactive element will shed its sub-atomic particles to try to become lead, a stable element. There are so many contrasts between the different physical and theoretical elements in society, and when these elements are disrupted, chaos quickly ensues until an equilibrium is reached again. During the French Revolution, the monarchy consistently failed to provide a standard of living to its people that is acceptable, and its government was failing. The price of bread rose from 8.5 sous to 14.5 sous in Paris which was 80% of a worker's wages.[9] During the Russian revolution, only a third of required food was making it into the cities and the

---

[9]Georges Lefebvre, *The Coming of the French Revolution* (Princeton: Princeton University Press, 1947), p. 98.

price of fuel quadrupled in Petrograd. Both of these circumstances caused a collapse in government and the rise of the people, but linking our understanding of hierarchy in society back to this rule of equilibrium, it is very interesting how in both of these cases a new political elite rose from the ashes of the peoples' revolutions. It further reinforces my point that an equilibrium has to exist and will restore and renew itself out of a period of chaos. In the case of France that came as Robespierre and later Napoleon and in Russia it was the Lenin and later Stalin. This shows that equilibrium works in hierarchical terms too, and the universe and societies will always try to come back to an equilibrium which satisfies the needs of the people with ruling class power, or the power of the elites in general. This is the same reason why radical changes to society are usually greatly opposed by the common populace, as they disrupt this equilibrium and the effect of doing this can be disastrous for the livelihoods of the people.

Providence continuously guides us through evolution and every single generation must survive a series of tests which strengthen the next, even if subconsciously. The struggles of one generation allow solutions to be found to those struggles which are then carried over into the next generation. These tests act like a disease on the human genome but in a psychological capacity not a physical capacity. When a body is attacked by a foreign entity, the spleen remembers its genetic code and builds white blood cells that resemble that same genetic code to destroy that entity. Each generation of human becomes more complicated than the next through these experiences. Providence is guiding us to be more like Himself and so the discoveries and life experiences of each generation are passed on to the next as human life becomes more complicated and the double helix that is history evolves and becomes more advanced.

Let's discuss some of these rules in action starting with divine extinction. The primary and most recognisable example of this can be seen in the ancient Roman civilisation. Rome had swallowed many cultures and nations throughout its eminence as an imperial power. It had used these cultures to enhance the strength of its own Roman identity and united many peoples under one shared “general will” as Rousseau suggested. He talked about how this "general will" was essential for a republic to remain stable despite diversity. A people that did not share a common set of moral, legal and civic values were destined for loyalty towards other ways of living and cultures which would create chaos. Rome successfully utilised its civilisational spine to absorb the negative effects of diversity while growing its ever-expanding tapestry of history and evolving into a stronger version of itself. An example of this can be seen in its absorption of foreign Gods. Upon conquering the Britons and making a new Roman province, the Romans established a new Britannic God called Sulis Minerva. She was a Britannic princess God who was commonly worshipped around modern Bath. This shows the Roman's ability to adapt to changing circumstances and is a perfect example of Edmund Burke's "change to conserve" principle. A civilisational spine represents these shared moral and legal principles in action. If these morals become too diluted with diversity, the spin will shatter, and chaos will ensue. Rome is a perfect example of this shattering and a delving into degeneracy through having a massively improved quality of life. By the end of the primacy of the Roman imperial era, there was constantly mass migrations from Dacia and Germania into Pannonia, Thracia, and Gaul. The imperial court struggled to handle these migrations only been successfully able to integrate a few foreign cultures into its civilisation, and the weakness of Rome became increasingly apparent due to its high quality of life, compared with those migrating peoples who were desperate to remove their own hardships through increased living standards. One of the cultures it successfully managed to integrate into its domain was the barbaric Franks in northern Gaul. However, other cultures like the vandals and Goths were extremely difficult to integrate due to their strength and Rome's growing weakness. Less than 10% of the army came from Italy during the late Imperial Era, highlighting how the increased living standards gained from being at the heart of a Mediterranean empire had weakened the resolve of these people. Instead the majority of the Roman Army came from the provinces, primarily Pannonia, Illyrica and Thracia, all border regions which were under constant threat of barbarian invasion. This further proves the idea that comfort can be the poison of a society as it weakens its societal core, whereas even small pieces of managed discomfort can drive a people forward through unrelenting grit and determination. This can even be seen on a personal individual basis. A person who grew up in difficult circumstances will likely be more resilient to challenges, be more independent and have a higher emotional intelligence than a person who grew up in a sheltered environment. This type of thinking has driven the “free-range kids” movement in the United States, which aims to re-assess traditional views of parenting that the more involved the parent the better and instead advocates for a freedom of children to discover the hardships of life on their own terms and find their own solutions. Thus, discomfort is definitely a positive attribute which can strengthen an individual and society if managed correctly. The point being here that Rome became too comfortable as an imperial power, in particular its core populace in Italy, and its inability to adapt to changing circumstances combined with its weakness allowed its collapse. Rome could not contend against the growing warrior culture of the Germanic tribes, shaped by centuries of warfare and harsh living. This also links back to the idea of equilibrium. When a society has too many resources and lives too comfortably its collapse becomes inevitable as its balance of equilibrium has been pushed too far towards comfort over advancement. This is what causes "divine extinction". Much of this chapter has been inspired by the Pennsylvania university professor, Johnathan Haidt. Haidt published a groundbreaking literary work on belief that has heavily contributed to the shaping of my ideology. Haidt developed the social intuitionist model of moral psychology and came to an understanding in his work, "the Rightous Mind" of why the universe must be in equilibrium. Haidt recognised that pre-conceived notions do exist, and rational thought comes after the pre-judgement rather than before. He then used this idea to explain why different types of morality exist between conservatives and liberals. Haidt described how equilibrium evens out both sides of the political ideology in terms of population based on numbers and action. Haidt described a series of life experiences which could shape the perception of an individual and form those pre-conceived notions and how we react rationally to them. He described how liberal democracy is good for humanity as it balances each side of the political spectrum with the other, thus producing a more stable society through pluralism.

Haidt used the example of leaded petrol in 1980s America to depict the universal rule of equilibrium perfectly. As the rise of neo-liberal economics began in America, the Democrats and Republicans sought very different approaches to the economy. The Democrats favoured a more centralised controlled economy with moderate government intervention while the Republicans began to favour laissez-faire principles. During Carter's administration, he allowed the Environmental Protection Agency (EPA) to begin a phaseout of leaded fuel from commercial consumption. After Reagan took power, he dramatically reduced the EPA's regulatory and legislative power, seeing it as a burden on business function. In fairness to Reagan, he was right. Quangos like the EPA can be disastrous for business and put checkmarks in the economy which can halt the upward trajectory of human evolution through a market basis, which is where most of human advancement originates from through technological innovation. However, the problem with this attack on the EPA is that it restricted the organisation's ability to phaseout leaded fuel quite significantly as it reduced its legal and legislative influence. Thus, while Reagan didn't stop the phaseout of leaded fuel, he did slow the process.[10] Under the Clinton administration, leaded fuel was officially made illegal in 1996 and the human effects of this regulation cannot be overstated. IQ would increase by 10 points over the next decade and crime

---

[10]Haidt, J. (2012). The Righteous Mind: Why Good People are Divided by Politics and Religion. Pantheon Books. (pp. 348 – 350)

would significantly reduce.[11] This is an example of a perfect political equilibrium. A yin and yan types situation. The socially liberal Democrats sought more control over the market to attempt to ensure equality of opportunity for all. The Republicans sought to enhance freedom through reduction in government control in the market. The clashing of both sides of the spectrum meant that the negative impacts of the phasing out of leaded fuel was minimal on business as it happened over a long period, and then by the time that leaded fuel was banned under Clinton, it had minimal effect on business operation as the phaseout had already occurred over a

---

[11]Reyes, J. W. (2007). *Environmental policy as social policy? The impact of childhood lead exposure on crime. The B.E. Journal of Economic Analysis & Policy*, 7(1), 1-43.

decade, but the human effects of this phasing out were phenomenal for the next generations. It is a perfect example of how liberal democracy, in particular the Republican Federal model can protect all interests through equilibrium of political parties in competition. In contrast, let's say that America was a one-party Democrat run nation, the phasing out of leaded fuel would likely occur immediately, as the government wouldn‘t need to answer to pressure from businesses and their owners. This could have a large effect on business, causing a slight economic retraction which could be devastating for businesses in certain areas, particularly the oil refinement sector. If America was a one-party Republican run state, the phaseout of leaded fuel may never have occurred, as environmental non-profits and quangos like the EPA could just be disbanded for the sake of allowing the market to do what it likes. This would of course mean the human condition was lower, and it would not be natural discrimination, it would be man-made discrimination as humans were responsible for the lowering of their own IQs and increase in crime despite their being an alternate solution which could increase the chances of millions of people to move up the great chain of being and become more like Providence. So, we can see that an equilibrium is not only necessary, but that the universe actively seeks it out. The idea of the Republican one-party state actively mimics governments throughout history that have not tried to maximise the liberty of their own people. The French revolution being a prime example of this, with the First and Second Estates (nobility and clergy) being removed from taxation while the Third Estate (the mercantile class, peasants, workforce and artisans) were all placed under heavy taxation. The ruling feudal elite suffered little from costly wars and projects. And this is mimicked in the Republican one-party state idea but instead of a feudal elite it was a capitalist elite. This shows how one-party states and autocracies can never last in history. In some cases, their decline may be slow, as they may have some benevolent rulers, but as the general population becomes more educated and humanity more advanced just like Providence these inequalities quickly become apparent and are resisted. This shows that equilibrium always will exist in the long and short-term and cannot be resisted, instead it should be accepted. In the idea of the Democrat one-party state we see a similar mimicry to the Soviet

Union. Lenin wrote in “State and Revolution“[12] during his exile in Finland in 1917 that he believed when the Revolutionaries took power in their respective states, the people would accept all their policies as they would recognise that they were acting in the working-class interest. Of course, this is not what happened at all because people are rational individuals who are primarily greedy and are not so altruistic. In the case of the Democrat state, a similar situation would take place, with an attempt to reach a truly Social Democrat state and mimic FDR‘s achievements in the wartime period. Over-regulation and government

---

[12]Lenin, V. I. (1917). *State and Revolution: The Marxist Theory of the State and the Task of the Proletariat in the Revolution*. Foreign Languages Publishing House.

involvement in the economy would take place which would reduce the effectiveness of the economy for those rational individuals which would result in national collapse over time. The balancing of both those ideologies into a competitive state, produced a moderate middle-path where government was responsible for all interests and where the benefits of both paths could be experienced by the populace. Next, we will assess inequality through the lens of truth and a basic thought experiment. This is an experiment that I have developed myself, inspired largely by the argumentation of Robert Nozick against John Rawls. I will label this thought experiment, "The Island of the Thousand". Let's imagine that a group of 1000 people were shipped to an island that had the perfect conditions of living. Every person worked their dream job, was paid the same, had the same car, the same housing, the same healthcare and the same education. All 1000 of the human population did not know each other, have prior information on the experiment or power over another person. Let's argue that there is no centralised government discrimination, and the government ensures perfect equality of opportunity. After a year of these conditions, some of the islanders may have invested money into local business which may have brought a return. Some may choose to start their own businesses through smart investment. Some may work excessively, jumping on this new start in life, working 80 hours a week. Some become leaders and compete for influence among the rest of the population. In contrast, some may not invest their money wisely or become comfortable with the idea of living in a completely egalitarian society with no major differences in access to resources. And so, inequality will quickly re-emerge. Why? Differences in ability, differences in desire, different priorities and different temperaments. Thus, the activity of attempting to regulate equality of opportunity at all times for all individuals to ensure fairness is nearly impossible and as it would require constant know how of personal circumstances from a government board or committee, similarly to how in the Soviet Union, a board of regulators was responsible for regulating over 24 million different prices.[13] A nearly impossible task. Then there is the moral

---

[13]Sowell, T. (2011). *Basic Economics: A Common Sense Guide to the Economy* (4th ed.). Basic Books. (pp. 123-125)

question of whether taking someone's wealth that they worked hard for and redistributing it lower in society is moral, especially if those people are poorer not out of natural discrimination, but man-made discrimination through refusal to work. Next, we will address the idea that life is sacred using a real-life example. After Hitler's blitzkrieg piercing into the French heartlands, the British and the French were faced with a dilemma of unhuman parallels. Over 300,000 loyal soldiers were stranded in Hauts-De-France with no escape and were entirely encircled by the Wehrmacht.[14] Strategically, it made very little sense to attempt to save these men. A rescue mission could've been

---

[14]Gardner, W. J. R. (2000). *The Evacuation from Dunkirk: 'Operation Dynamo', 26 May–June 1940.* Routledge.

massively costly to the royal navy and preserving desperately needed fuel for a prolonged war made the most strategic sense. And yet, Winston Churchill and his war cabinet decided to save them, despite the huge risks. These were the souls of Britain and France and Churchill decided to save them to preserve the nation's fighting spirit. This decision was not made out of military rationality, but a basic recognition that life is more important than all other principles including questions of justice (should others have been rescued?), questions of equality (as some groups were prioritised above others) and questions of fairness (like the fact many French troops were left behind). It was the saving of these British souls that Churchill prioritised above all else. Even when it meant violating principles of justice to rescue priority groups or contradicting utilitarian reasoning, the decision to save human life was still chosen. And who in their actual moral and right mind would say what Churchill did was wrong? This simple question shows that under pressure, societies will abandon all of their prized principles except one, the saving of their own and the upholding of life, showing beyond doubt, that humans can recognise the value of life through the lens of truth.

We must also address an extremely important point here. Weakness from any individual to a society is the equivalent of death. What I mean by this is, while I myself am a libertarian and completely believe in individual choice, your choices should not be supported or rejected by the state. If you refuse to work or cannot afford your bills, you cannot expect the state to bail you out. That is not what the state is there for. The state is there to defend individual liberty and taking money off others to make up for your own personal mistakes is not liberal. Its feudal. Thus, through libertarianism natural selection takes place. Weak people, weak attitudes and weak ideas die, leaving only the strongest people and ideas left to push humanity on an upwards trajectory.

So now let us look at where this path will end for human evolution. The more advanced whole civilisations become through the spiral of history the closer we get to providence and his level of being. And so, the ultimate human achievement would be to conquer death. Humans can create, feel joy and procreate and yet we die, leaving behind a legacy or not. It is death that stops use from being the most god-like and in the future, with advancements in neurobiology and advanced robotics, it is entirely possible humans may conquer death, breaking free from evolutionary need. The lifespan of a species is measured in relatively easy terms. A species seeks to improve its own circumstance against other tribes or species by conquering the best living spaces that can provide the most resources necessary for producing life. A species does this as it recognises it not only wants to end its own hardship by improving its quality of life, but it needs to ensure the survival of its legacy by producing offspring, and in order to do this it needs to secure a sufficient and reliable source of resources. This is an area which modern society is uniquely bad at, we have access to a nearly abundant pool of resources and yet we cannot turn those resources into offspring, just like in the rat experiment. Thus, this is what I mean when I say that we can break free from evolutionary need.

PROVIDENCE
GUIDES US

A Pattern in History

History follows a set pattern. It is a double Helix and as time goes on, it becomes more and more complicated as possibilities and life progress.

"What we do now echoes in eternity."
— Marcus Aurelius, Meditations

Throughout this chapter we will first assess the theories of other historians with a similar outlook to my own cyclical view of history. These historians will include Oswald Spengler, Arnold Toynbee and even Ibn Kaldhun. We will establish a new theory of history as accurately as we can with historical examples and explanations.

Oswald Spengler wrote the second volume of his great work "The Decline of the West" in 1922 after the devastation of the Spanish influenza and the First World War. He focused on the separation between culture and civilisation as a model for lifestyle which would be expanded on in further works by Amaury De Riencourt. Spengler's core theory in decline of the West was the idea that civilisations are living organisms which have a life cycle of birth, growth, peak, decline and death. He argued that this was not an exception but rather the rule. The culture of a civilisation was focused on art, beauty and aesthetics. This culture was full of energy for religion and growth. He then argued that from this, could arise a civilisation which was far more concerned with maintenance of its imperial possessions through expansion of bureaucracy, a death of creativity and a greater emphasis on technological advancement rather than beauty. History was not linear, it was an endless cycle of birth, death and renewal. In his view, the West was entering the final stage of this lifecycle and was in decline.[15] This

---

[15]Spengler, O. (1926). *The decline of the West* (C. F. Atkinson, Trans.). Alfred A. Knopf. (Original work published 1918–1922)

perspective cannot be seen as surprising when considering the horrors that Western civilisation had just experienced through tantamount death. His view of history therefore must be approached cautiously as his view of history may have been influenced by the poor state of society and politics during his era. His research may fail to properly assess the impact of modern-day technology on history and his theory of life-cycles as he was writing during a time of great technological change, but before key human inventions like the micro-chip in 1947 had been achieved which would alter human history forever and change society. I believe Spengler's ideas are the closest we have to truth. His ideas are very worthy of merit and should be taken seriously despite the largely negative outlook influencing his work due to the time period in which he was writing. Spengler did not just look at the West as an example of a birth and death cycle but many over civilisations which further reinforces his point. Spengler used two primary case studies of "high cultures" to show his lifecycle theory. The first of his theories was ancient China, in which he argues that the chaos which engulfed China after the collapse of the Zhou dynasty, was not coincidental. He argues that the feuding and warring states that emerged after the collapse of the dynasty were primary examples of the growth of a new civilisation experiencing growing pains and competition which would push them into a uniform culture which would become a civilisation. His second example was the Greek city states during the Peloponnesian War and classical Greece. He saw the competition between the warring states as an essential step towards civilisation, as the cultures competed to outdo each other, creating a strong Greek identity. This, he argues, lead the Greek states to reach their philosophical and cultural apex. In both of these cases, creative turbulence precedes political centralisation, which to Spengler proves the lifecycle of civilisations. However, Spengler's work has not been without criticism from other historians. Herbert Albert Laurens Fisher criticised Spengler's view of history as it didn't have empirical evidence by which a culture or civilisation could be measured, "Men wiser and more learned than I have discerned in history a plot, a rhythm, a predetermined pattern. These harmonies are concealed from me. I can see only one emergency following upon another as wave follows upon wave".[16] However, this view seems simplistic because it doesn't consider wider issues which encompass history. His view is radical in the sense that it doesn't allow room for manoeuvre and has an almost nihilistic outlook on history. He refuses outright to look at the patterns of history which are clearly apparent in the works of Spengler or consider his argumentation. The reason behind this is almost certainly that Fisher was an elite Oxford educated liberal he saw these types of theories as an ideological threat against free choice. He was deeply immersed in Victorian liberal traditions and there were many theories of history at this time including Karl Marx's

---

[16] Fisher, H.A.L. *A History of Europe.* London: Edward Arnold & Co., 1935. Preface.

socialist theory of history. So, it may have made more ideological sense for Fisher to have rejected these types of explanations behind history to suit his own ideological desires rather than accepting that most of Spengler's works are good observation. My personal response to Fisher is that I recognise the ideological need for him to dispute patterns which can influence ideology and damage choice. However, I would remind him that human action is not purely random. People aim for key objectives during their lifetimes, and this should not be ignored. People aim to belong as detailed by Johnathan Haidt in the Righteous Mind in his "Hive Mind" chapter, people aim to improve their own lives by increasing living standards, and people aim to do what is best for themselves. This is the basis of liberal thought, galvanised by the Industrial

Revolution as a political reality. The idea that there can't be patterns to history is therefore a fallacy because the aims of each generation are roughly the same, despite the process getting there being different as humanity becomes more complex. As a person who believes in personal choice and the Fourth Way, I believe that the theory of natural selection applies to society and that the state should not get in the way of this process, as a classical liberal like John Stuart Mill would argue. And so, while individuals are free to pursue their own goals of improving their lives and maximising their own well-being, this pursuit may indeed produce patterns among each generation as the goal is the same. No one is born wanting to have a poor quality of life or achieve little to nothing in the time they are here. This idea is explained extensively in the book "The Worm at the Core" by Sheldon Solomon, Jeff Greenberg, and Tom Pyszczynski who argued in favour of a Terror Management Theory.[17] The book details the idea that the fact of mortality is known by all humans and is a point of subconscious terror for individuals. They argue that in order to try and evade death, humans have adopted some psychological methods to overcome fear. One of these methods is loyalty to a religion or nation. Thus, we can see here how patterns through looking primarily at individual human psyche could emerge as this terror of death encompasses all living humans to have existed. Humans long to be a part of something larger than themselves, a

---

[17]Solomon, S., Greenberg, J., & Pyszczynski, T. (2015). *The worm at the core: On the role of death in life.* Random House.

nation, a movement or a culture. This is then passed on to the next generation as another coping mechanism developed by human during evolution was having children. The idea of recreating another version of yourself that will live on after your death settles the human psyche and gives a sense of invincibility. We can see that these patterns passed on to each generation, therefore, may produce wider historical patterns, as the ambitions of individuals do not change due to human evolutionary psychology. Humans strive to conquer death and in doing so support a culture. Through generational work this culture then becomes a civilisation through pursuit of similar goals. Therefore, where Fisher went wrong was not in his political beliefs themselves, but in the failure to recognise that humans share similar values no matter there geography, and it is liberalism that allows these pursuits to be achieved by individuals who compete, while those who lack motivation and passion are left behind. Another criticism of Spengler's work is that it is vague and tends to cherry-pick different civilisations from history to prove his point while ignoring others that may not fit into this rule. My personal argument against this is that critics who espouse this argument are looking at history in too rigorously. History is like economics and is not the same as physics or mathematics. You cannot take a snippet of time from history where a nation may not fit into Spengler's theory and claim that it doesn't work. The lifecycle of all nations is different. Some are extremely short and some are extremely long. The birth of a new culture may happen in decades and then suddenly collapse, before reemerging. The point I'm making is that history is more nuanced than simply looking at all events as objective realities that must follow a set pattern of understanding. Of course, there are truths to history that shouldn't be twisted or ignored, but we cannot push aside a functioning and realistic theory that explains human evolution simply because the pattern may vary at times, though is still the same overall. As we will see later with an investigation of Amaury De Riencourt's expansion of Spengler's work, history is never set in stone, but that doesn't mean patterns cannot emerge. Overall, Spengler's works and argumentation are solid. They are supported by modern psychological theories on the individual and how this effects wider society as well as being grounded in truth.

Next, we will assess the idea of Arnold Toynbee from his work, "A study of history" wrote in 12 volumes over 3 decades.[18] Toynbee differs from Spengler's idea that the birth, life, death cycle cannot be avoided. Toynbee largely acknowledges the same cyclical nature of history as Spengler but argued that death wasn't inevitable and could be avoided with necessary reform and effective response to outside stimuli. Toynbee argues, "civilisations die not from murder, but from suicide". His theory of how the pattern emerges goes as follows:

1. Genesis: a creative minority will respond to an

---

[18]Toynbee, A. J. (1946). *A study of history* (D. C. Somervell, Ed. & Abridged). Oxford University Press.

innovative political, technological, societal or economic problem effectively and as a result the majority will follow them.

2. Growth: the civilisation will experience immense growth and unity, sharing massively similar parallels with Spengler's theory of a "culture".

3. Times of trouble: There will be a breakdown of order and a series of troubles which appears to be the end of the apex of the culture, similar to the feuding states of China and Greece in Spengler's theory. The idea that struggle enhances creativity and civilisation to new heights of unity.

4. Universal State: This is the stage in which bureaucratic centralisation takes place and Caesarism emerges. In this stage, the state becomes more controlling and authoritarian. This idea is the exact same as Spengler's view of the civilisational rise out of the chaos of a culture in decline. It is worth noting here that there is another theory of history that places wider emphasis on the actions and influence of singular individuals as an explanation behind history. This theory, named "The Great Man Theory", was championed by Thomas Carlyle in the 19th century as an explanation of the path of history. He used influential

figures like Caesar and Alexander the Great as an explanation of the driver behind historical events. The main problem with this theory, which the Fourth Way is aiming to grasp with is that it ignores cultural and contextual issues which can produce these types of figures and so is short-sighted.

5. Disintegration: Creative response to external and internal stimuli fail and produce decay of a civilisation leading to death.

Through analysis of Toynbee's work we can see his view of history is much less rigid than that of Spengler. Instead of seeing death as an imminent reality, he argues that it is not always the final result, and it can be avoided if the ruling classes find a viable solution. The problem with this theory is simple. Going back to my earlier point on history being more nuanced than a mere snippet in time, the problem with this theory is that one generation of a century long empire may solve an immediate problem which can lead to a long-term problem that then has to be faced by the next generations and could be disastrous. How can you balance Toynbee's theory that the creativity of the ruling class minority in dealing with problems over time is the determining factor in whether a civilisation will collapse, when some problem span generations of different individuals who are a part of that same class and potential may have different solutions to problems than previous generations, or even new types of knowledge on these problems. An argument must therefore be formulated which can support Toynbee's theory while also acknowledging the nuances of history. The answer is relatively simple and is grounded in truth. Creative failures are still creative failures. It may be true that future generations of an empire in decline may not understand the constraints opposed upon them by previous generations of the ruling classes, but this is the course of Empires. Toynbee's point is that creative failure, no matter if it spans generations and cannot be blamed on a singular action is still creative failure and will lead to a collapse of the civilisation. Toynbee is not aiming to produce a scientific experiment with variables but is instead aiming to understand the past in a nuanced and intelligent manner without forming contradictions. Critics of Toynbee point to his writings being around the 2nd World War and use this to explain his criticism of a supposedly “civilised Europe”. His life experiences undoubtedly may have influenced his view that technological advancement does not equate to moral progress. However, I think this idea as a criticism of Toynbee is incredibly weak as it actually led him to profound historical insight of the paths of civilisations. He was able to recognise in an era of massive technological change that this progression does not help civilisation become more great, instead it was social and moral cohesion that encouraged this. He recognised that the most technologically, intellectually and philosophically sophisticated civilisation on the planet was able to inflict such destruction on itself and thus this was proof that greatness does not extend from innovation but from moral and spiritual cohesion. I believe his experiences shaped a belief in creative moral leadership and so should not be discounted just for being wrote in a particular environment. This links back to the metaphysical civilisational idea of the Fourth Way that a spine which holds together myth, morality and identity exists and forms the foundations of civilisations and a weakening in this spine causes chaos. Several historians were critical of this view of history, primarily Edward Hallett Carr. Carr rejected Toynbee's theory as being philosophically vague and lacking methodology. Carr accused Toynbee of producing a moralistic sermon rather than an actual theory of history. He claimed Toynbee's work was filled was vague metaphysical terms like "creative minority" which were hard to define in practice.[19] Carr instead argued that history should be entirely based on specific empirical facts rather than on a law of philosophy. He essentially claimed that Toynbee's moral ambition outweighed his historical methodology, producing a false deduction of matters. The problem with this argumentation from the perspective of Carr is that it is overly reductionist and narrowest. If we looked at history only from the perspective of empirical evidence the conclusions we would come to would be faulty as they would not be built of any foundations of why the history happened, instead we would be left with a series of facts with no explanation or nuance behind them. The investigation of history is not just what happened but

---

[19] Carr, E. H. (1961). *What is history?* London: Macmillan. pp. 10–11, 89–90.

why it happened, and this is the idea the Fourth Way and academic historians like Toynbee and Spengler aim to assess with clear methodology while also acknowledging the nuances of history with its many twists and turns. Overall Toynbee's work can be seen as being immensely valuable and reliable as an investigation into history. The ironic aspect of his work is that he describes himself unknowingly. While critics can argue that Toynbee's views were shaped from a negative perspective of Western civilisation post the 2nd World War, the reality is that he actively embodied his idea of a "creative minority". Yes, his views were established from the perspective of having survived an implosion of Western culture, but his response and investigation into history as a result of having lived through this period is both morally creative and philosophically creative. Thus, not only are his works valuable for historical investigations but he accidently embodied his own theory. The Fourth Way is philosophically aligned with Toynbee in the sense that it builds on his works. E.H Carr may argue that terms like a "creative minority" or too vague in practice but as we covered in the previous chapter, we attempted to establish the real Great Chain of Being which does allow for movement between states of being. Thus, the Fourth Way philosophically aligns with Toynbee's view of history that a creative minority first solves a major problem in society, causing the masses to follow as the Great Chain of Being rule of the universe recognises this hierarchy of meritocratic talent.

Next, we will examine Amaury De Riencourt's great work, "The Coming Caesars" wrote in 1957.[20] De Riencourt's approach is hugely similar to Spengler and Toynbee's, but it approaches the question of what causes decline differently to either historian and he sees the end result of a civilisation's lifecycle differently from either historian. De Riencourt entirely accepts the lifecycle theory and the rough stages developed by the previous two historians. It is the reasoning behind each of those stages that is different. De Riencourt does not believe that decline in civilisations is caused by cultural exhaustion like Spengler or that it is caused by the creative failures of the elites like Toynbee. Instead, he mixes

---

[20] de Riencourt, A. (1957). *The coming Caesars*. New York: The Viking Press.

both views to produce a new conclusion, that the real answer is institutional and cultural decay in democratic societies. Amaury is suspicious of too much power concentrated in too few hands but also recognises that tyranny of the majority can destroy whole societies. He argues that as democratic equalitarianism grows in the West like it did in Rome in the late republic, it will lead to a mass coercion of the people against rational thought and towards emotional reasoning. He argues that this will produce Caesarism, as one charismatic leader will come along and sway the masses into tyranny. In some aspects, De Riencourt aligns with classical liberal thought, a fear of tyranny of the majority and a breakdown of national values of a big government and constitutionalism. However, he mimics the Founding Fathers in his works and the senatorial republicans of ancient Rome as he believes in the need for a ruling elite to guide the masses. He believes somewhat in an aristocratic class and therefore cannot be considered to align fully with this school of thought as he rejects democracy as a civic virtue and is heavily critical of mass democracy. His view of history is also very cynical rather than open minded. So ideologically, I would consider De Riencourt a classical republicanist. On purely ideological grounds, I cannot support De Riencourt's views. I believe in democracy of all people that are a part of a nation. I do agree that there must be a system in place that prevents tyranny of the majority, but this system was produced 250 years ago with the founding of the American nation. The electoral college purposely ensures that the smaller states within the federal republic have a higher vote total in proportion to more densely populated states. This was done with the intention of ensuring the urban elite couldn't dominate politics due to their numbers, and that the interests of moral rural Americans would be listened to. Riencourt's idea that there must be some sort of aristocratic class is not necessarily accurate as this could greatly hinder the evolution and upward trajectory of humanity as well as upset the universal rule of equilibrium as one elite class can make decisions for the rest of the population. His views may have been influenced by his own bloodline and family as he was a member of the French nobility. Despite the French nobility having lost their influence after the French revolution, their bloodlines still lived on and Riencourt represents one of these bloodlines. It is entirely possible he may have yearned for a return to when the nobility had influence due to his own bloodline. However, one area in which I can agree with Riencourt is in the idea that liberty must be preserved through truth alone. There can be no illusions and disruptive mediums that blind perception of truth from the reality. Authoritarian figures are damaging and disrupting to liberty as they often spread overly false or emotional tales of injustice or decline to win influence among the people. This type of behaviour should not be tolerated and there must be a vocal opposition against this type of manipulation to ensure true liberty can always be achieved. If what the popularist is saying is true, then that within itself shows a breakdown of government function or liberty which must be fixed to put an end to popularist poison. A historical example of where this type of action should've been taken but failed can be seen in the late Roman-Republican era. The optimates (bureaucratic conservatives) were the anti-corruption and pro-traditionalist political party. They sought to embody the Mos Maiorum and traditionalist Roman attitudes of a life built on rural agrarian values. The problem with this attitude is that Rome had changed far too much from its founding as a small agrarian republic to a Mediterranean superpower. The refusal of the traditionalist optimate faction to extend the franchise to the masses and remove a broken voting system as well as end systemic corruption proved fatal for the republic. As much as Caesar was a tyrant, he was also right. The republic was breaking down and democracy was failing. The ruling classes were not adapting and Roman society was falling apart. Its urban hubs were becoming over-crowded as the countryside elite bought up masses of land and filled them with slaves, forcing Italian workers into the cities. The truth of what Caesar was saying allowed him to rise to power. Even though the intellectual elites argued day and night in speeches and in writings that Caesar's pointing out of the truth was false for a wide array of ideological reasons, the truth does not care about ideology only about reality. And so, the masses of Roman's followed Caesar as he did not need complex ideological argumentation for what he and the Roman people saw so clearly, that the Republic was dying. This allowed him to do heinous things that were undemocratic without any repercussions from the electorate who still loved him. Caesar deliberately tried to undermine the legislative process by bypassing the senate at all time and taking his bills directly to the public assembly. His mobs terrorised senators and their families who did not support Caesar, with his proconsul Bibulus being assaulted in the streets by Caesar's mob as he protested against Agrarian reform. But this argumentation also pokes a hole in De Riencourt's thinking. It was this enshrined political aristocracy that caused the collapse towards Caesarism not mass democratic equality. The exact same thing can be seen replicated in many civilisations throughout history, including in revolutionary France, during the English civil war and in pre-ww1 Russia. Had members of the senate like Cato, Cicero and Ahenobarbus pushed through meaningful reform to maximise liberty like electoral reform and commissions against slavery in the countryside, Rome may not have fallen into the hands of a tyrant like Caesar. Rome as a civilisation may also have lasted longer, as democratic ideas and principles would've allowed free debate and utilised the knowledge of the entire Roman electorate to solve complex issues, rather than the knowledge of a small traditionalist minority. While I disagree with De Riencourt's sentiment of anti-democratic nature, I do recognise that the breakdown of democratic institutions can occur, but the response to this isn't to limit the franchise, it is for intellectuals to maximise truth. This shouldn't be truth driven by ideology; it should be truth driven by reality and changes to government should be made to accommodate that truth. Overall, De Riencourt's view of the franchise is problematic. I do not support his undemocratic sentiment or expression of the need for an enshrined ruling class of sorts. This is not the moral basis of the Fourth Way. The class you are born into means nothing in the Great Chain of Being. The essence of being a human is your life force. What you do with that life force is what determines your closeness to providence, and place on the Great Chain of Being, not what family you were born into.

We will now come to a comprehensive overview of all three historians' opinions to come to a reasoned conclusion about how history works. Spengler's view can be defined as historical determinism, that all nations throughout history follow a set path which is inevitable. Toynbee's view of moral historicism reflects the idea that it is the spiritual and moral choices which may determine whether a civilisation will collapse, while accepting Spengler's lifecycle theory. Riencourt's view can be defined as civic fatalism, or the idea that as democracy grows tyranny becomes more likely through emotional manipulation of the masses. Here is the reality of the theory grounded in truth. Civilisational collapse is inevitable, but not in the same way as Spengler claimed, it being metaphysically determined. Spengler's assessment of the lifecycle of civilisations was correct, a carefully curated rhythm that moves from spring to winter and from flowering to exhaustion. And yet, his determinism can be considered too rigid and too fatalistic. Collapse is not necessarily the same as fate, but it often is the same as consequence. It is not pre-written, but born from accumulated failures, missed challenges, and the slow erosion of meaning and form. Toynbee understood this nuance of history that Spengler failed to recognise. I have purposely spoke positively in my earlier analysis of Spengler because he developed the structure and lifecycles by which a peoples rise, peak and die, but I cannot agree with his determinism. Toynbee recognised that civilisations fall not by accident, but by failing to respond creatively to challenge. Civilisations can be saved if even for a short time, or as long as a centuries by process of spiritual renewal, bold reforms to society, or the reawakening of a unifying cult. And so, collapse is not prevented, it is delayed. This delay can matter greatly. The longer a civilisation preserves truth, coherence, order, and honour, the more it can shape the arc of human history, and feed what comes after. However, even with perfect responses, the slip-ups are inevitable. No human system can preserve clarity and virtue forever as humans are imperfect. Civilisation is always tending toward entropy. Despite this inevitability, the Fourth Way does not represent a nihilistic perception of history, it represents hope and purpose. As Amaury de Riencourt rightly observed, the ashes of fallen civilisations do not vanish, they are repurposed and carried into the future. The ruins of one fallen civilisation become the bricks of another. The Roman Empire may have died, but its corpse nourished Christendom; the Classical world collapsed, but its philosophy seeded the Renaissance. Every fall carries within it the raw material for the next ascent. Evolution uses death as a vehicle for advancement by learning from the past. It recycles the fragments of the dead and binds them into a higher synthesis—more ordered, more conscious, more divine. This is where the Fourth Way can be considered to depart decisively away from De Riencourt's civic fatalism. Riencourt sees a terminal trajectory, from liberty to Caesarism to decline and death, but the Fourth Way sees a spiral, not a circle. All civilisations may fall, but what emerges from it can grow upward, not merely repeat the mistakes of the past. The death of one order fertilises the next. And those who live within late civilisations are not merely witnesses to decay; they are midwives of rebirth. Thus, the end of a civilisation is not the end of history, it is a phase in the story of evolution's slow, upward climb toward the complexity of providence. Civilisations die, but history ascends. Collapse is real, but so is transcendence. The task of the Fourth Way is to accept the impermanence of all human orders, while working to extend their life by refining their purpose and preserving their greatness, so that from their ashes, something greater may be born.

Several key examples of the Fourth way model of history can be seen in the real world. The late Roman Republic and Roman empire embodies this idea perfectly. The Republic collapsed due to conditions detailed earlier in this book and it led to the rise of a dictatorship, just as all three analysed historians would describe. Then the Empire adopted hundreds of reforms over centuries that would help delay its collapse. Cultural integration like the invention of Sulis Minerva and the administrative reforms of Diocletian and Constantine helped continue the empire for centuries longer having defeated internal and external threats to their civilisation. Though Rome did collapse eventually just as Spengler would say was inevitable, there was an accumulation of mistakes over centuries which led to this decline that if they had theoretically not happened, may have resulted in a modern Roman Empire. However, Riencourt's view that civilisations die and provide the fertiliser for future civilisations can be seen intently in the adoption of Christianity in Europe and Greco-Roman civic values in the American constitution grounded in republicanism. In addition, another example of the Fourth Way model can be seen in the collapse of classical antiquity. The old world of literature, art, beauty and imperialism collapsed with the death of antiquity. A new rural civilisation emerged known as the dark ages with social fragmentation and intellectual decline. However, from the death of antiquity we can see a revival under the Carolingian intellectual renaissance which was then replicated in other nations. The philosophy of law and governance were once more studied by the elites which helped build a new culture which would eventually become western civilisation which we are still currently living in today. At the court of Alfred the Great, the learning of Roman history, poetry and literature was demanded of the all the nobility's children, so that the future leaders of the realm would possess the lessons of the past. Alfred's learning directly mimicked that of Charlemagne's France as his grandfather had been an exile on the mainland for decades before becoming king of Wessex and was close to Charlamagne. This revival of antiquity thinking and its influences on western civilisation today show the impact that a one dead civilisation can have on the present culture being developed into a civilisation. Look at ancient Greek thought as an example. Greece was known for despising authoritarian rule and tyrants. Even city states with kings would overthrow their kings if they thought they were too tyrannical. These sentiments are still present in western civilisation today, with democracy being the most popular form of governance in the west.

The following describes the pattern of history according to the Fourth way with all possible caveats:

1. Chaos: There is an era of human regression

2. Rebirth: out of this regression grows a culture of order and shared moral values

3. Expansion: The culture/nation grows in size and population (in the modern day via industrialisation), accumulating more political thought and knowledge of reality.

4. Cultural decline: internal and external threats become a problem for the expanding culture and civilisation and one of two things can happen: complete death (Alexander's Macedonian Empire) if this happens the lifespan ends here as a premature life, political innovation from the elites (Prime-minister Asquith's war

against the House of Lords in the UK) in which case the cultural expansion will continue until fall into authoritarianism (most likely outcome as the nation rallies around the populist and an imperial era begins)

5. Imperial Era: civilisations rapidly expand and become the dominant culture in their spheres of influence but suffer from authoritarian dictatorship and suppressed liberty.

6. Imperial decline: the elite ruling class becomes too comfortable and degeneracy sets in. This causes creativity against internal or external threatening stimuli to be reduced.

7. Death or continuity: The elite either solve the threatening

influences or don't. This can result in either a continuation of the civilisation or its divine extinction.

We will now look at an alternative view of the theory of history that is entirely not cyclical in nature but rather linear. Karl Marx detailed an entirely new perspective for his age on historical theory, but its linear nature leaves it open to easy rebuttal. Marx claimed in his work "The Communist Manifesto" that history was entirely driven by economics. All other ideas that make up human nature like politics, religion, society and culture were epiphenomena of economic systems. History, in his view, was concerned primarily with a class struggle and not with social or cultural issues. This was his "superstructure" idea that there was the soil of economics, and the tree which grew out of the soil was everything else that makes up a society, from art to politics. So Marx would argue that economics determines society, and the existence of the feudal church was to support the feudal landowners, while the existence of bourgeoisie liberalism defends property rights which were key to maintaining bourgeoisie power. In his mind, ideas were reflections of material interests not truths within themselves. From this perspective he produced a set of stages for historical development:

1. Primitive Communism: tribes share their resources to survive.

2. Slave societies of antiquity: the oppressed were the slaves.

3. Feudalism: the nobility oppresses the serfs and peasants for their own advancement.

4. Capitalism: the bourgeoisie oppresses the proletariat for material advancement.

5. Socialism: the workers rise up and overthrew the oppressive rich creating a socialist state.

6. Communism: the workers destroy all elements of a capitalist society. Money is gone and states evaporate.

Marx believed that these stages of history would be followed exactly with the end result being Communism.

However, there are several major problems with Marx' linear economic theory. First off, reality is much more complex than simply being grounded based around one source.[21] Economics or similar arguments for linear history like divine intervention and will, do not recognise the truths of history or its causations. They are too reductionist in their approaches and do not link trends through history nor how events from other aspects of the human condition may have influenced other spheres. An example of this can be seen in the works of historian Max Weber, who investigated the evident link between the Protestant reformation and the rise of

---

[21]Marx, K., & Engels, F. (1848/2004). *The Communist Manifesto* (S. Moore, Trans.). Penguin Classics.

capitalism.[22] Weber correctly recognised that the Calvinist ideas of pre-destination provided the spirit of Capitalism. Religion was no longer based around your piety or nobility in the church but around proving that you were chosen by God to be saved. In order to show your holiness and God's favour of yourself you had to succeed in life through material wealth and growth while outcompeting your rivals. This would show that God had chosen you before birth to be saved, rather than being saved through obedience to the church and tradition. This investigation by Weber reveals two things. First, that the reformation had an effect on how economics was perceived, as mercantile

---

[22]Weber, M. (1905/2002). *The Protestant ethic and the spirit of capitalism* (S. Kalberg, Trans.). Roxbury Publishing Company.

attitudes became more celebrated because of the need to appear as in God's favour, thereby showing a direct religious effect on economics. Second, it shows that economics isn't the only influence on society, as new attitudes towards what it means to be successful and what became socially acceptable changed as a result of changing religious attitudes. To take a step back and just analyse linear historical thought for a moment, this is the main problem with its foundations. It takes into account some truths but does not acknowledge wider historical context as to not weaken its own argumentation. Therefore, one of Marx primary explanations behind his historical theory, that of a "superstructure" cannot be taken seriously in practice. There clearly millions of interlinked social, artistic, religious and cultural events that influence every other category of the human condition including economics. Critics of my argumentation may backtrack and argue that Protestantism did give rise to capitalism, or admit that there are millions of inter-linked cultural, religious and economic events that wouldn't make sense if you removed one from the other, but they may say that this doesn't prove Marx is wrong, this is just a part of the evolutionary class struggle he described and his theory shouldn't be discounted for this inconsistency. However, I would argue that this way disregard of Marx' own theory of linear history and acceptance of inconsistencies essentially mean that his theory entirely reduces the complex textures of human life into on variable which cannot be considered analysis, it is dogmatic and the same type of thinking you would see in a most radical sect of an Abrahamic religion. It also means his theory is entirely not robust as it explains everything, even contradictory evidence to the whole theory as being a part of a wider picture. If Marxist want to accept that Calvinist thinking did drive new spiritual attitudes towards wealth creation but then argue this is a part of a wider theory despite it being contradictory, their theory is immune to disproof and is therefore religious in nature. Perhaps this does explain why Marxist's see human nature as perfectible and believe in a Utopian state of society. There are also many problems surrounding the period in which Marx was writing which makes his theory problematic. He was writing at the height of industrial revolution Britain when the workers were poorly treated and lived in inhumane conditions. Marx' work would have no doubt have been influenced by his own personal experiences of witnessing massive human misery and suffering. He likely aimed to understand this turmoil by using his intellect to formulate an engineered form of history that would produce a utopian end result. This is a common theme with linear historians in general. They tend to simplify history to understand principles outside of their realm of knowledge or to explain suffering with the hopes that things will get better as time goes on and the workers will find justice in Communism. In other words, real history does not influence their thought, their thought influences their history. They attempt to adapt socially constructed ideas to a historical framework in hopes of predicting something larger and better than their own minds and that of the state of society. The cyclical view of history developed over a century of political and historical thought and adopted by the Fourth Way recognises the nuanced nature of history and does not aim to make it fit into ideological basis, instead it monitors the truths of history and comes to a reasoned conclusion. The problem with Marx and linear historians is that they treat history like a machine, when it is an organism.

So, to summarise this extensive explanation behind world history, the Fourth Way builds on cyclical historians works, primarily Spengler, Toynbee and De Riencourt to provide a reasoned judgement of how history repeats itself. This in turn adds to the evolution of mankind as we become more advanced. The Helix of human history continuously grows and adapts to more conflicts as we become more advanced.

On Building Society

Sociology is the backstage of society, behind the red curtain of the theatre reveals the machinery of society.

"Liberty cannot be established without morality, nor morality without faith."
— Alexis de Tocqueville,
***Democracy in America* (1835)**

Sociology is a fascinating topic. It is the politics behind politics. It investigates how society functions and why it functions in the way it does. However, there are major problems with the entirety of sociology as a science. It has been tainted heavily by misconceptions and untruths. Many sociological theories place much emphasis on left-wing perceptions of equality, particularly idea of morality being subjective and right-wing thought which is often grounded in truths is criticised as being too amateur. The problem with sociology is that it is the epitome of left-wing university intellectualism, who develop socially engineered ideologies which would not work in real life, and at times actively defy truth. This may be seen as harsh by members of the field, and I want to note sociology is an absolutely spectacular science that can help in explaining reality, but I am going to be brutally honest here, most theories are wrong. The fourth way will analyse functionalism, post-modernism and a new sociological theory I will call Civilisational Selection Theory. We will critique the other methods of sociology in this chapter as well as building on the Fourth Way perspective. I will then go on to explain Fourth Way views on key aspects of society, from education to policing.

First of all, we will assess post-modernism as a sociological theory. Post-modernism rejects what it calls, “metanarratives”,[23] or in other words ideologies that aim to explain everything. Grand theories like Marxism or the evolutionary political philosophy established in this book have no place in reality according to a post-modernist sociologist but instead there is no truth. They argue that application of grand theories marginalises alternate voices and enforces a singular truth. We will re-address this point later on as it is blatantly false. Post-modernists also accept relativism as a truth, while rejecting all other truths, which within itself appears a philosophical fallacy.[24] Relativism explains that truth is entirely

---

[23]Weber, M. (1905/2002). *The Protestant ethic and the spirit of capitalism* (S. Kalberg, Trans.). Roxbury Publishing Company.

[24]Lyotard, J.-F. (1984). *The Postmodern Condition: A Report on Knowledge*, p. xxiii.

subjective to culture and the environment in which you are raised. It explains language and culture shape our perception of reality and thus we cannot find moral truths. Lastly, they believe in a hyper-reality, enhanced by a media saturated world, where our perception of what is true is shaped by images, signs and brands.[25] There are several major flaws in this theory of sociology. We will use philosophy and truths of reality to disprove this way of thinking. It should be noted that this theory is a continuation of the type of indirect realist versus direct realist argument we addressed earlier in the book with the pink elephant example. While the Fourth Way recognises indirect realism presents

---

[25]Foucault, M. (1980). *Power/Knowledge: Selected Interviews and Other Writings 1972–1977.* Pantheon Books.

a dangerous temptation, the temptation to abandon the pursuit of truth in favour of comforting relativism, the conclusion that post-modernism reaches as a result of its belief on indirect realism is wrong. It is defeatist in nature and doesn't try to reach a conclusion on truth, instead it argues for its subjectivity. Instead of identifying reality as subjective, we should instead recognise that indirect realism enhances truth and actively proves it. If all cultures see the world differently, the question is not whether truth exists, but which perception aligns best with objectively reality. A just society will aim to maximise truth, in order to allow for rationalism on an individual basis to flourish and for a recognition away from emotion and towards independent thought. A healthy society will teach its people not to dissolve truth in relativism, but to strive to maximise it. Through rigorous education, open discourse and competitive innovation, acquirement of a singular truth will emerge through time, not by the decrees of other voices, but by testing and challenging. This is the primary difference between post-modernism and civilisational selection theory. Post-modernism states that our views are filtered and so truth is unknowable, whereas the Fourth Way argues that our views can be filtered, but because of this truth is harder to reach, but when we do it's hugely valuable and enhances our liberty. Truth, in this ideology, is the key to rationalism not its death. A post-modernist rebuttal to this argumentation would be that my pursuit of an objective truth is still culturally embedded and I have not proved that my own values, methods or world views are privileged over any other. But once again, we see the nihilism and defeatism present in post-modernism, the Fourth Way does not reject that our perceptions are filtered by language and experience, but to argue that there is no truth beyond these constructions is silly. A window filled with condensation cannot be considered the same as a blindfold. The truth does exist, and we should seek to reach out by a natural selection of ideas grounded in truth, not dissolve reality into relativism. The presence of media that may distort our worldview does not disprove truth, you need the intellectual discipline to see through it. Another major contradiction of the philosophy behind post-modernism was briefly touched on earlier, a post-modernist may argue that "there are no universal truths" but the problem with this is that it is a declarative statement within itself, and so cannot be a truth, thereby reversing its own statement and proving that there are truths. Let's also look at this from a mathematical perspective, with a very basic statement, 2+2 cannot equal 5. Now a post-modernist critic would argue against this by saying that mathematics is a closed system and this is a short-sighted view on human experiences. They would say that using mathematics is a rhetorical trick to make the Fourth Way seem undeniable when societies don't run on formulas they run on culture and language. However, the problem with this critique is that maths isn't a closed system. Planes stay in the sky, apartment don't collapse, and cars move all because of mathematics. If you tried to alter the maths, these things wouldn't work anymore and chaos would ensure, as ignoring truths leads to chaos. Another problem with the rebuttal of post-modernism on the mathematics statement is that it is contradictory. You can't claim that there is even a singular universal truth like mathematics and then continue to claim there are no truths because you've actively proven through admission that mathematics is a truth that there are truths. Another problem with post-modernism is the unfortunate background of its founders which definitely influenced their life experiences. The father of post-modernism Jean-François Lyotard was a Marxist in his early life but resorted to post-modernism due to the horrors of the Marxism in practice.[26] His nihilistic approach to reality and rejection of an ideological truth likely shows emotional disillusionment rather than accurate

---

[26]Baudrillard, J. (1994). *Simulacra and Simulation*. University of Michigan Press.

deduction. Another father of post-modernist thought was Michel Foucault who lived an openly gay life in a highly conservative France.[27] His views may therefore have been hindered hugely by societal and institutional discrimination because of his sexuality which could have altered his world view away from a set morality and towards a deep distrust of authority or traditions. We can therefore see how the perspectives of each sociologist were likely hindered by their own personal experiences, which is not only an active contradiction to their own theory, as their views towards truth were likely affected by cultural norms but also explains their defeatist and nihilistic view of the world.

---

[27]Megill, A. (1985). *Prophets of Extremity: Nietzsche, Heidegger, Foucault, Derrida*. University of California Press.

Next, we will look at functionalism as a sociological theory. Functionalism treats society as an organic whole with limbs, not too dissimilar from the Fourth Way's idea that society is an organism. Functionalists see these limbs as the different traditions and institutions that keep society together. They see a system of equilibrium, where if one limb fails, the other limbs step in to make up the lost ground. Functionalists believe society functions best when the people share common values and norms. These values are then passed on by socialisation through the nuclear family or education. Functionalism is inherently Conservative valuing tradition and continuity as a basis for a stable and healthy society. An example of the pursuit of stability sought by functionalists can be seen in Talcott Parson's view of the nuclear family.[28] Parsons argues that the nuclear family has two primary role:

1. Primary socialisation: This is the idea that the nuclear family is that first and primary overseer of a child's development. The nuclear family, in his view, exists to instil within children the knowledge of what is socially acceptable in wider society.
2. Stabilisation of adult personalities: The nuclear family provides emotional support to its adult members. This helps them cope with the stresses of daily

---

[28]Eribon, D. (1991). *Michel Foucault.* Harvard University Press.

life, known as the “warm bath theory”. To Parson, the role of the family is to therefore maintain social cohesion and stability through providing a stable and nurturing environment for all its members. Parson also expressed that the mother and father of the family have different roles due to biology.[29] The husband was the leader of the family and the worker, while the wife was the caregiver and nurturer, highlighting the inherent traditionalism of Functionalism. I will first start by saying that functionalism is respectable as a sociological

---

[29]Parsons, T., & Bales, R. F. (1955). *Family, socialization and interaction process*. Glencoe, IL: Free Press.

theory, though as we will soon discover it has flaws. Firstly, I recognise the need for social cohesion is paramount, as without cohesion, the civilisation spine of myth, culture law and identity may collapse. This also aligns with functionalist views that society must have a shared consensus of values. However, the main issue with functionalist ways of thinking as that its aversion to difference will create stagnation. A society with complete uniformity of all its element will of course be stable, but it will not thrive. The evolution by natural selection of the best ideas can never rise through the popular mindset because there is a pre-established way of thinking that cannot be challenged. And so, the Fourth Way agrees that structure should exist, but only to pursue truth, excellence, and innovation, not be stuck in outdated social morals. This brings me to a criticism of Parson's idea of the nuclear family. Its emphasis on the need for a family to be entirely nuclear with a man and wife and kids is within itself problematic, as his justification for it ignore other realities and thus come into conflict with truth. Firstly, I agree with Parson that a nuclear family type model is necessary for social cohesion. A child should have two parents figures instead of one and should be nurtured. This is entirely because children who are not raised in this type of environment often produce negative outcomes. 85% of youth prisoners in America come from a fatherless household and boys raised in a household without a father figure are more than twice as likely to commit crimes.[30] Of course, there are many other factors that play into this increased likelihood to commit crime, and I don't deny that. The loss of a source of income coming into the household from another parent figures would naturally increase economic hardship which could lead to an increase in primary

---

[30]Parsons, T. (1956). *The American family: Its relations to personality and to the social structure.* In T. Parsons & R. F. Bales, *Family, socialization and interaction process* (pp. 3–33). Glencoe, IL: Free Press.

deviancy. However, regardless of these other factors, the idea remains the exact same. A family needs two parental figures not just to produce a healthy learning environment for children but also to properly care for their children's needs financially. However, one area where the Fourth Way rejects the functionalist premise of family is in the idea that other types of family shouldn't exists as they are a threat to social cohesion. It is perfectly normal and desirable for a gay couple to have and raise their own children. We should not stop homosexual couples from raising their own children or building a life and a family simply because they don't fit into a male or female category of what a family should look like in the functionalist perspective. In addition to this principle, functionalism also seems to rule out older types of family traditions which can still be seen primarily in Asian countries. For example, there is nothing morally wrong with the extended family model, and actually having the wisdom of older generations around children may not be a bad thing. My point against functionalism here is that its worldview can be too narrow and reductionist to the point that it risks embalming society with tradition, mistaking uniformity for peace while causing stagnation and even possibly negatively affect social cohesion in the long term. Betty Friedan perfectly summarised this view in her great work, ”The Feminist Mystique” where she rightly pointed out the ”problem that has no name”.[31] She explained how women were becoming frustrated from constantly being domesticated in a confined space and were taking this frustration out on their children and husbands, directly contradicting the ”warm bath” theory. She recognised females as being rational individuals who should have a say in the direction of their own lives, rather than simply following the status quo. We will touch on this idea a little

---

[31] Friedan, B. (1963). *The Feminine Mystique*. New York: W. W. Norton & Company.

later in the economics section, but she was right. The domestication of women prior to them entering the workforce removed half of the knowledge and brain power of the general population. This shows how the Fourth Way contradicts functionalism in the sense that it recognises the need for change. The Fourth way aims to build a civilisation of rational individuals who compete in society and as a result produce a sharper civilisation. Functionalism on the other hand, believes that society should maintain social cohesion above all else which can hinder competitive progress and the spiral of human evolution. Functionalism builds a well-oiled machine. The Fourth Way aims to build a living organism, one that adapts and ascends.

Now we will look exclusively at the sociological theory presented by the Fourth Way: Civilisational Selection Theory. The Fourth Way recognises society as being a fluid and ever-adapting organism, just like history. Social institutions and structures are not inherently flawed or ideal but should be adaptable and fluid, capable of constant adaptation to changing circumstances. Social institutions should be grounded entirely in truth through empirical knowledge of truth. Ideology should never have an influence over social institutions as these act as an indirect realist medium that distorts our reality and therefore makes true liberalism of the individual harder to achieve. Social institutions must be unbiased and grounded in reality to be truly adaptive to outside stimuli; the institutions must be able to properly adapt to outside pressures and debate to maximise individual liberty. They must aim to maximise the liberty of the individual through encouraging debate, criticism and intellectualism. Institutions should also always promote truths over lies. All public policy in institutions like healthcare, policing and even in educational circles should be peer reviewed and extensively debated by all parties involved. It is important politically that left wing and right-wing identifying university professors exist in their respective departments to assess balance and produce higher quality work closer to truth. This belief is similar to the Systems Theory in Sociology but differs from this theory because it is more dynamic and evolutionary. We place great emphasis on the individual and their chance to achieve individual freedom and complexity. We accept that there will always be a stronger and weaker class in society. The weaker class are free to pursue their pleasures and disregard hard work, but should expect to be bailed out by social institutions and systems like the welfare state. Instead, their life decisions are directly responsible for their outcomes and regardless of the personal character of a person, we should not allow empathy or loyalty to ideology cloud our judgement of these issue and lead our societies into untruths. A person's life outcomes should be acknowledged as being entirely of their own making. If a teenager does awful in high school during their exams because they drink with their peers every weekend or have poor behaviour in school, then this is their fault even as an adult. We should not aim to try to fix their mistakes of the past or give them a second chance, as a part of them will always have this internal attitude of rebellion, rather than aiming to maximise their understanding of reality. If they could not take their education serious in school, society should not be expected to help them in the future as this is a burden on the advancement of civilisation. I want to say here I am not arguing that this type of life should be out of bounds for members of a nation. You have the absolute right to live your life however you choose, but that is your decision, and society shouldn't have to bail you out for your mistakes. I am not saying that a person should never be given the chance to fix their lives if they are in a bad state. I am not saying that a person who was rejected from university due to bad grades should not have the chance to improve their grades and try again, but I am saying that you shouldn't rely on anyone for that pursuit, instead that should be funded by yourself not the state. Civilisation Selection Theory sees social institutions as being changeable. The positive aspects of a government department or service should be maintained while the negative aspects are removed, regardless of whether or not this will damage bureaucracy confidence in government. The primary aim of this sociological theory is to drive society towards a brighter future and towards the pursuit of truth. Some may ask something like "well you've discussed truth a lot in this book, but who determines truth" and the answer is simple but most reading this are not going to like it. The answer is reality. If basic biology describes that a man cannot be a woman, then attempting to change reality is not a true maximising of that person's liberty. In fact, it is illiberal because it denies truth and therefore is unreal and we know that liberty can't exist in untruths. Individuality by means of liberty cannot be fully achieved when the truth is not apparent. Which bring me to the next idea, "what about situations where the truth is unknown?" The answer to this statement is complex but does exist. We should aim to unlock the truth through innovation and experimentation, and by allowing for the expression of ideas by means of liberty. Ideas which are a burden to society should be rejected by the populace and through rationality will be. So, what do I mean by this? Well let's use the example of Eugenics and racism. Of course, as we discussed earlier these are forms of man-made discrimination. In his work, "The Genetics of Human Populations", Richard Lewontin disproved the artificial theory of race. He claimed that the most genetic diversity in human populations is actually between individuals and not groups. 85% of genetic differences were found between individuals with only a 15% variation occurring between groups.[32] The Human Genome Project highlighted on this even further with better technology proving that genetic differences between individuals were less the 0.1%. A blonde-haired blue-eyed Swede nearly

[32]Lewontin, Richard A. (1972). *The Genetics of Human Populations*. Columbia University Press, p. 5.

shares the entire genetic material of a sub-Saharan African. The HGP put the final nail in the misconception of race, and yet till this day there are still racists in all races who insist on starting a race war. Firstly, this is perfect example of what I mean when I say ideas grounded in truth should be accepted, while those that aren't should be entirely rejected as they contribute to stagnation of society. However, going back to my original argument, the Jim Crow laws of the South severely hindered liberty and individual freedom, thus not allowing for black people to have a chance at success in society. This idea was even further proven in the racist IQ tests of 1910s America. Lewis Terman developed a system of measuring IQ we still call today the Stanford-Binet test. He used these tests on people of all racial backgrounds and came to the conclusion that anyone who wasn't of northern European ascent was less intelligent and therefore genetically inferior. Of course, these tests were absolute nonsense. The test items were based on experiences of White-middle class families or knowledge that was familiar to White-middle class families. These included knowledge of Western culture and history producing a huge cultural bias in the tests. Of course, this meant the poor and those of a different race scored much lower than the White mostly Anglo-German American middle classes. These types of discrimination are man-made and not based in truth and so are illiberal. Therefore, we must ensure that our experimentation and competition of ideas is grounded in entirely in truth. These IQ tests claimed to be grounded in science and claimed to be accurate but were not. We must be wary of science that is not accurate as it leads civilisations in pursuit of dangerous ideology. In addition, the Jim Crow Laws are a blatant violation of personal liberty and did not allow black people to rise through the hierarchy meritocratically, thus limiting societal evolution. We must abandon illiberal untruths or beliefs in society that limit competition. While I have talked extensively about racial discrimination, it is clear that the long term effects of this discrimination are still apparent today and that positive discrimination, particularly in university opportunities should occur, specifically if the individual from a minority group is poorer and those past discriminations are still apparent. I am not therefore contradicting my earlier point that the state shouldn't try to regulate equality of opportunity because I don't believe it should, but I do believe that when it comes to education which is of immense importance in the Fourth Way we should take into account all aspects of an individual's situation. In the Fourth Way truth is paramount, and institutions must be shaped by evidence not ideological beliefs. We should aim to foster institutions that avoid ideological dogma and abstract political thought and look at empirical evidence and human behaviour. When abstract ideas are pursued in these areas, chaos ensues. Lastly, of course, Civilisation Selection Theory believes that societies evolve over time and civilisations grow strong. We must pursue different ways of thinking and compare those ideas not just in subjects like science, but in literature, politics and history to come to rational conclusion about what is the truth, which is unshaped by ideology. Of course, the Fourth Way recognises that human though is often flawed. At times it is impossible for those who can think less critically to separate political dogma from reality and truth. Cognitive biases affect individuals' ability to evaluate information objectively. These biases can lead to the rejection of evidence that contradicts their pre-existing beliefs, creating mental filters that distort the truth and therefore prevent true liberty. In the context of society as a whole, this means that ideologies or false beliefs can become entrenched, and the collective decision-making process may be swayed by irrational thinking. A relevant and perfect example of this can be seen in political polarisation. Many hardcore feminists on the liberal left see gender as nothing more than a social construct by espousing support for thought experiments like this: A child grows in a facility where there is little difference in facial structure, clothing or body types between male and female workers and the child does not have "gendered toys" and is not educated on differences between male and females. Would this child still have the same outlook on gender when released into the real world as another person? The problem with these types of thought experiments is that they have been tried by sick individuals. Bruce Reimer was born in 1965 in Winnipeg Canada as a twin. During a circumcision procedure, the boy's penis was severely damaged and left unable to function properly. His parents Janet and Ron took Bruce to see Dr John Money who was employed at John Hopkins university. He was a famous gender theorist and sexologist at the time. Money told the family that since the boy's penis was damaged, they should have him undergo a sex change and raise him as a girl, and this is what the family did. During this period there were several strange behaviours noted by the parents of the biological male. Despite never being told of his past or birth gender, the boy stood up to urinate even though he had a vagina. He showed great interest in playing with his brother's toys and did not like the feminine toys that his mother and father had given him. As he grew into a teen he began wearing masculine clothing and behaving in masculine ways. Eventually, the newly named Brenda began suffering with depression and became suicidal. By 14, he entirely rejected the female gender and believed he had something wrong with him before his parents told him the truth. His case was flaunted all around the US by Dr Money as a success story for his gender socialisation theory, even the suffering he caused on such an innocent family was paramount and evil.[33] Eventually, Bruce ended his own

---

1. [33]Colapinto, J. (2000). *As nature made him: The boy who was raised as a girl.* HarperCollins.
2. Deke, J., & Haimson, J. (2013). *Evaluation of the Knowledge Is Power Program (KIPP) in middle schools: Impacts on achievement and other outcomes*. RAND Corporation.
3. Tuttle, C. C., Gill, B. P., & Borman, G. D. (2015). *KIPP middle schools: Impacts on achievement and other outcomes*. Mathematica Policy Research.
4. Renzulli, L. A., & Partee, G. (2010). *KIPP's impact on high school graduation: Evidence from a national sample*. Journal

of Education for Students Placed at Risk, 15(2), 145-169

5. Tuttle, C. C., Gill, B. P., & Borman, G. D. (2010). *The long-term effects of the Knowledge Is Power Program (KIPP): Results from a national study*. Journal of Education for Students Placed at Risk, 15(1), 24-39.
6. Pew Research Center. (2025, May 8). *Republicans have become more likely since 2024 to trust information from news outlets, social media*. Pew Research Center.
7. Kuklinski, M. R., Briney, J. S., Hawkins, J. D., & Catalano, R. F. (2012). Cost-benefit analysis of Communities That Care outcomes at eighth grade.

Prevention Science, 13(2), 150–161.

8. Cyranoski, D. (2023, March 8). *Scientists create mice with two fathers after making eggs from male cells*. The Guardian.
9. Rice, W. R., Friberg, U., & Gavrilets, S. (2012). Homosexuality as a consequence of epigenetically canalized sexual development. *The Quarterly Review of Biology, 87*(4), 343–368.
10. Vasey, P. L., & VanderLaan, D. P. (2010). An adaptive cognitive dissociation between willingness to help kin and non-kin in Samoan fa'afafine. *Psychological Science, 21*(2), 292–297.

11. Blanchard, R. (2018). Fraternal birth order, sibling sex ratio, and sexual orientation of men and women: New tests of the revised theory. *Frontiers in Psychology, 9*, 446.
12. Rice, W. R., Friberg, U., & Gavrilets, S. (2012). (Same as 41)
13. Guillamon, A., Junque, C., & Gómez-Gil, E. (2016). A review of the status of brain structure research in transsexualism. *Archives of Sexual Behavior, 45*, 1615–1648.
14. Rametti, G., Carrillo, B., Gómez-Gil, E., Junque, C., Zubiaurre-Elorza, L., Segovia, S., ... & Guillamon, A. (2011). The microstructure of white matter in

male to female transsexuals before cross-sex hormonal treatment: A DTI study. *Journal of Psychiatric Research, 45*(7), 949–954.

15. Burke, S. M., & Anderson, A. K. (2014). Gender identity and the brain: A functional perspective. *Neuroscience and Biobehavioral Reviews, 40*, 1–13.
16. Guillamon, A., Junque, C., & Gómez-Gil, E. (2016). (Same as citation 45)
17. Hare, L., Bernard, P., Sánchez, F. J., Baird, P. N., Vilain, E., Kennedy, T., & Harley, V. R. (2009). Androgen receptor repeat length polymorphism associated with male-to-female

transsexualism. *Biological Psychiatry, 65*(1), 93–96.

18. Gore, A. C., Chappell, V. A., Fenton, S. E., Flaws, J. A., Nadal, A., Prins, G. S., ... & Zoeller, R. T. (2015). EDC-2: The Endocrine Society's second scientific statement on endocrine-disrupting chemicals. *Endocrine Reviews, 36*(6), E1–E150.
19. Gore, A. C., et al. (2015). (Same as citation 50)
20. Lukianoff, G., & Haidt, J. (2018). *The coddling of the American mind: How good intentions and bad ideas are setting up a generation for failure*. Penguin Press.

life. The point of the story here is simple. These types of abstract ideas that are normally pursued via religion dogma often cause catastrophe. Many feminists on the left to this day still argue that gender is a social construct, despite the fact there is biological and empirical evidence to suggest that is not the case. This example shows that critical thinking is often clouded by ideological bias. The Fourth Way argues that social institutions should verify truth without bias based on empirical and real-life evidence and allow for free speech. If an ideology does become accepted by a society that is wrong, it will upset the natural equilibrium of the universe and disrupt the civilisation spine. These types of ruptures quickly become apparent like a leaking pipe in a bathroom. And then how the creative minority solve the issue will determine the fate of that civilisation. If the creative minority or ruling classes fail to end the untruth it will lead to an eventual collapse of civilisation as untruths spread causing society to become less innovative and competitive, whereas if the creative minority solve the problem, which they can only do through full acceptance or partial acceptance of the truth, then the civilisation may be entirely saved until a new problem emerges or if only partial, just for a time. Re-touching on our assessment of political polarisation and biases can reveal a new idea that truth which is not fully known is dynamic, and so total rejection of political ideology in pursuit of truth is also not entirely required. What I am saying is that Civilisational Selection Theory believes in critical thinking, and before the entire truth is unlocked, we must treat it as dynamic, and as new information comes to light, we must accept it if it is empirically correct. It is in this case that political polarisation may become an issue. If one side of the political spectrum is correct, it may give them more credibility in the eyes of the electorate, causing the opposing parties to solidify their positions even more and accept untruths as reality. This is a case when civilisation selection theory would demand that parties and institutions change with ever changing information which brings us closer to the truth.

Before continuing, we should address potential rebuttals of my sociological theory. There are 3 primary rebuttals which could be cited from this work, thus I have made a separate section for these rebuttals so that we can use empirical evidence and truth to debunk them. The first and most likely common critique will include the idea that subjective experiences of an individual or group may shape political ideology and thus our understanding of what is right or wrong. Critics might argue that relying entirely on empirical evidence might discount the complexity of the human experience. However, my response to the critique is that the truth is dynamic when it is not known and that the Fourth Way does not reject subjective experiences but instead requires social institution to adopt objective evidence. Individuals in any case are free to support and hold any beliefs that they wish, but verifiable facts must be the basis of social institutions and public policy, because this allows administration, which is the best for all of society, not just a few. A perfect example of this is the issue of vaccination. Many do not like themselves or their children to be vaccinated due to anecdotal stories of the dangers of vaccines. This belief is completely fair and a key aspect of that person's individual liberty as well as competing ideas in the marketplace of thought, but public institutions which can verify that vaccines are safe should not adopt these untruths and begin describing vaccines as unsafe if all the empirical date points towards the opposite. Or in other words, you are free to hold ideas that are against empirical evidence, but public institutions should adopt verifiable facts as the basis of their policy. I would also like to say that the Fourth Way does absolutely not reject subjective experiences as forming the basis of what we understand to be true.

If an adult who was raped as a child advocates the death penalty for paedophilia, they naturally have a strong argument for the case as the actions of that individual have violated John Stuart Mill's harm principle and may act as a deterrent against potential criminals. However, if a black man was beaten by four white police officers and advocates for the disbandment of the police in government, that is clearly chaotic and a policy doomed to failure, as we have seen the effects of living without a police force in pre-1829 London. Thus, we can see how subjective experiences are incredibly important to investigating the truth, but they must also be analysed by cause and effect on society as a whole and public institutions should adopt the truth as this is what is best for society. Experiences in the crime cases mentioned above must be analysed by their potential effects on society and how they will help or hinder sovereign individuals. Other critics may argue that Civilisational Selection Theory oversimplifies views towards social mobility. They may argue that meritocratic systems are good but do not account for the difference in circumstances that each individual may have in their lives. My argument against this is clear and simple. The only time the state should ever be involved in ensuring equality of opportunity is in education and healthcare because these two things directly pertain to a child's success. A child cannot do well in school if they have a psychological condition that cannot be treat without a doctor or a physical condition that may hinder the child's chances of success. All children should have access to education and tools to help them thrive. This should include positive discrimination where grades are concerned for the poorer in society. How they use these tools however, to provide a better future for their own children or themselves than what their parents had is their own prerogative. We will touch on education a little later in much detail. The next argument a critic may formulate is that the welfare state is good at reducing inequalities. While this may be true in some cases, it makes the functionalist mistake of arguing for social cohesion and tranquillity over evolutionary competition. A society where the government takes responsibility for it failed citizen's actions is not liberal in nature but is socialist. Instead, the state should ensure that welfare is available in the form of opportunities for jobs and chances for self-improvement like college and skill courses.

I'm now going to go through different social institutions piece by piece to present Fourth Way views of social institutions. We will first start with education. Education is massively important to Fourth Way ideology. The government should play a direct role in ensuring education is accessible to the entire populace from being old enough to go to school. It should be the law that every member of society must attend school, regardless of mental health or physical issues. As of writing this in the United Kingdom in the year 2025, some teachers will argue that school are under-funded, and I don't necessarily disagree with this but our outlook on how school should work must massively change. Schools in the UK and in many western nations are broken due to bad behaviour and robotic teaching that lacks passion. The best environment to encourage a child to work hard is one in which his peers and superiors work just as hard and adopt a strict learning culture. We must make education environments play a role of discipline and learning once again within our society and the positive aspects of this change can be seen in the results of the Knowledge is Power Program in America during the 90s. The measures taken by the schools were as follows:

1. Longer School days (7:30am while 5:00pm)
2. Summer learning programs to keep students engaged during breaks
3. High academic expectations from a young age. There was an adoption of a

dictatorship of benevolence in the schools, where teachers promised to get their students into the best universities while expecting good behaviour.

4. There was rigorous discipline, not just of students but of staff. There were constant checks on lessons and increased school department centralisation. Student were given an immediate punishment for bad behaviour but could be awarded for doing the right thing. Bad behaviour was not just punished with punitive measures but also through a form of rehabilitation where a chat was scheduled with a counsellor to correct the behaviour. There were no

exceptions to the rules, and they always remained consistent.

The results of these types of measures were outstanding. According to a study in by the RAND Corporation in 2013, KIPP schools consistently outperformed their age group on standardised tests. KIPP students scored the top 20% of national averages in maths and 25% in reading after attending the program for 3 years.[34] A study by Mathematica found that students were 0.4 deviations above their peers in their math skills. In reading they were 0.2 deviations higher. These both show that despite being in lower income areas, the KIPP school system can provide a

---

[34] Colapinto, J. (2000). *As nature made him: The boy who was raised as a girl*. HarperCollins.

gateway for greatness.[35] A 2010 study found that KIPP students graduated from high school at a rate of about 80% compared with the 60% national average.[36] This same study showed that 56% of KIPP students went on to attend college compared with just 30% from the surrounding communities.[37] All of this evidence points to the fact that a school which takes itself more seriously achieves better outcomes and it doesn't

---

[35]Deke, J., & Haimson, J. (2013). *Evaluation of the Knowledge Is Power Program (KIPP) in middle schools: Impacts on achievement and other outcomes*. RAND Corporation.
[36]Tuttle, C. C., Gill, B. P., & Borman, G. D. (2015). *KIPP middle schools: Impacts on achievement and other outcomes*. Mathematica Policy Research.
[37]Renzulli, L. A., & Partee, G. (2010). *KIPP's impact on high school graduation: Evidence from a national sample*. Journal of Education for Students Placed at Risk, 15(2), 145-169

matter what kind of a family you were born into, all that matters is the quality of education and what the individual chooses to do with it. It is in this spirit that the Fourth Way believes that this strategy should be adopted by all schools across the country. Schools should not be grounded in ideological biases but should encourage critical thinking in the classroom. This is a key aspect of education in my opinion. There should be classes of debate and discussion that fuel intellectual curiosity and allow the market of ideas to flow. Any teacher that actively aims to censor class discussion or impose their own viewpoint as the absolute truth, when the truth hasn‘t been unlocked on a particular issue or if what the teacher is saying is grounded in untruths and biased thinking, they should be investigated for misconduct. The school should also be responsible for discipline and crime prevention. There are many ways this can be done, and all require extra funding from the state to build a truly elite school system. I will now make a list of items that I believe are necessary to rebuild social cohesion through the school:

1. School day changes: 9 am while 2pm for primary school children and 9 am while 4pm for middle school (secondary school) students. High school students (sixth form/A levels) should attend school from 10 am while 6pm.
2. The school day for high school students should consist of an hour drill exercise each day on the school field or in the gym. Students who refuse to do this should be punished accordingly.

There should then be 2 lessons of an hour long with a 5-minute break in the middle and a 30-minute break after the 2 hours. There should then be another 2 lessons following the same pattern of a 5-minute break between each lesson. There should then be a 20-minute form period followed by a 2 hour supervised revision session. One of these weekly lessons should be based around nutrition and health.

3. For high school students: there should be a 1-hour drill exercise session upon arrival to school. There should then be a 3-hour supervised study session. There should then be a 1-hour free time period, in which extra-

curriculars can be attended. There should then be 3 lessons held on the subjects of the pupils with a 15-minute break between each.

This is not a be all and end all but it is what I perceive to be a perfect model for development and learning of a child. The exercise drills are designed to give time for the children to exercise in a way that doesn't disrupt their revision at home and to keep the general population fit. We will address the nutrition classes later on under our health section. To the Fourth Way, school isn't just about getting the best grades, it is about providing structure to society and improving social cohesion. In terms of how school should work, I believe the American grading system is much better and fairer than the UK model. I believe we should adopt a GPA system over a prolonged period of education to truly give the individual the best chance they have and to provide a realistic outlook on the academia of an individual. One of the safest ways to ensure accurate results in science is to run your experiment many times over and analyse results, rather than accepting or rejecting hypothesis based on one experiment. We must instead allow students to prove themselves over a long period of education. Universities then have the best assessment of a student's outlook based on a time period. I think GPA should begin in middle school, what we would call GCSE stage. How this is worked out is not to be determined by myself, but I do think this is a rough outline of how the system should work.

Next, I will look at the role of freedom in society. Free speech is absolutely fundamental to the functioning of a civilisation as we have already discussed many times, but we must now look more closely at ideas of free speech, the media and policing to investigate freedom. The social contract is a good idea and prevents us from falling into chaos. Most accept this, besides anarchists who are not grounded in truth and have no plan to build on society except personal greed. We will start with the media. The media plays an increasingly pivotal role in public opinion, yet it can be extremely biased. This problem is less prominent in the United Kingdom where news agencies are regulated against political biases. The Fourth Way believes that this should be adopted globally as part of a removal of political biases from social institutions. News agencies and media should report on all stories, not matter the party or ideology in power and they should be unbiased in their coverage of the news. Articles should not be more or less lenient on a political party simply because the writer supports them. Equally, the media must be truthful and honest. I believe that a system of fines for biased media should be in place just as it is in the United Kingdom. The people should formulate their own views on political, economic and social issues, that are unhindered by a group of intellectual elites at a London broadcasting station. These measures aim to maximise rationality in the pursuit of liberty and individual freedom, as well as avoiding groupthink. According to a Gallop poll in the United States conducted in 2021, 81% of Democrats describe the media as trustworthy while 53% of Conservatives describe the media as trustworthy.[38] This difference should not be that surprising considering that political polarisation is at a whole new level of divide compared with the 80s. I'm not going to go through examples of this as it is blatantly apparent when watching CNN versus Fox News. Both agencies blatantly report the news through their own political lens when this is not their job. They will not report serious stories about political figures if they support their views but will report on stories of political figures who do have differences to them. Critics may argue that this is the

---

[38]Tuttle, C. C., Gill, B. P., & Borman, G. D. (2010). *The long-term effects of the Knowledge Is Power Program (KIPP): Results from a national study*. Journal of Education for Students Placed at Risk, 15(1), 24-39.

role of a free media, but as we've already established freedom cannot exist without truth. Purposely being divisive is not truthful, its corrosive and it should be neutralised. This brings me to the next idea of free speech. There should be absolutely no limitations on free speech unless it incites racial or religious hatred. If you want to protest outside of parliament there should not be any limitation on that. If you want to criticise government publicly and openly you should do it without consequence. If you want to propose a radical new idea in your educational institution you should absolutely do it. When there is a control over the market of ideas it creates chaos and stagnation. It can lead to the collapse of a civilisation in its entirety if it is not solved. Had Rome adopted democracy after the fall of Claudius and returned power to a more stable and fairer senate than prior Caesar, it is entirely possible that the Italy and Europe we see today could've been drastically different. Rome may have survived, if not its empire, its civilisation in Italy. The market of ideas forces people to think freely and choose their own path based on rationality and egotistical individualism. The best ideas then survive and became part of human civilisation. Ideologies that try to limit human thought when they take control of nations are destined to die. The Soviet Union is a primary example of this. Now we will look at the balancing of the social contract by re-assessing the role of the police in society. Politicians often run on simplistic plans like increasing the number of police officers during their time in power. The problem with this is that it doesn't solve the issue of why people are committing crime. This

is an area my education strategy aims to fix. Discipline needs to be re-integrated into schools and a sense of achievement, aspiration and community must be restored. Through increasing the quality of education and providing stability to a child or young adult's life, I am aiming to reduce deviant behaviour due to poor socio-economic background. In addition to this, I believe strongly that a re-introduction of local community centres that can provide services like therapy and communal workshops is necessary for social stability. Crime is a defiance of the shared general will and the law, which threatens the civilisational spine. We should aim to reduce crime at all costs but simply hiring a massive amount of police officers is not the solution to stopping crime. A program in the United States called
the "Communities That Care" program

opened youth community centres and provided CBT to teens with troubles. By the 7th grade, teens were 25% less likely to initiate deviant behaviour and by the 10th grade teens were 17% less likely to engage in deviant behaviour.[39] This shows the value of these types of programs.

We will now look at other aspects of society in this section which are primarily concerned with the homosexuality and transgenderism. It has now been almost widely accepted in the heartlands of the West that sexuality is a part of a person's identity and

---

[39]Pew Research Center. (2025, May 8). *Republicans have become more likely since 2024 to trust information from news outlets, social media*. Pew Research Center.

shouldn't be controlled or regulated by the state. There are still countries in which this isn't the case and I will talk about this issue here. Gay people have rights. It is their human right to have sexual relations with whomever they wish, to marry who they wish and to raise their own children, no different from a heterosexual couple. There may be homophobes who will suggest that this goes against my own moral philosophy of truth above all else as they will argue that two men cannot procreate and thus it is biologically wrong. However, this isn't a breakaway from truth because two men living together can still have and raise their own children via means of a surrogate and new technologies are making it possible for male only parentage. Scientists in Japan created offspring mice from two male fathers.[40] Another problem with this theory is that, as of writing this book in 2025, the increasingly likely explanation behind homosexuality appears to be epigenetic causes. This is a field that is still under much research, and even if it is wrong, my stance will not change as being gay is not a choice, thus we cannot punish a group of humans for something they didn't choose but it is beginning to appear as if homosexuality is a process of birth. Epigenetics refers to the process of heritable genes being turned on or off by tags, like methyl groups. Some studies have suggested that sexually antagonistic

---

[40]Kuklinski, M. R., Briney, J. S., Hawkins, J. D., & Catalano, R. F. (2012). Cost-benefit analysis of Communities That Care outcomes at eighth grade. *Prevention Science, 13*(2), 150–161.

epigenetic marks may be passed on during the process of growth in the uterus which will alter genes sensitive to testosterone.[41] This alters how the brain responds to different sex hormones and likely induces homosexual behaviour in later age. Biological reasons for this are still being assessed but one reason is the caregiver theory. There is an evolutionary theory that a woman will have a gay child to help with the raising of other children in their own family or even tribal community and contribute to social cohesion. There is small amounts of evidence that suggest that stress during pregnancy is more likely to trigger these epigenetic tags, contributing to this theory that a gay

---

[41]Cyranoski, D. (2023, March 8). *Scientists create mice with two fathers after making eggs from male cells*. The Guardian.

child is born to add to social cohesion.[42] This type of behaviour has been observed in the tribes of Samoa and is known as the fa'afafine effect. This theory may be further supported by the fact that statistically, younger brothers are increasingly likely to be gay as the family of older brothers grows (about 28% to 33% increased likelihood per older brother which as baseline, for a son with no brothers would mean they have about a 3% chance of being gay which then increases by 33% per older brother so the next brother would have a 3.9% chance and so on).[43] Another study in

---

[42]Rice, W. R., Friberg, U., & Gavrilets, S. (2012). Homosexuality as a consequence of epigenetically canalized sexual development. *The Quarterly Review of Biology, 87*(4), 343–368.
[43]Vasey, P. L., & VanderLaan, D. P. (2010). An adaptive cognitive dissociation between willingness to help

2012 suggested that this epigenetic marking may exist as it also boosts female fertility.[44] There is evidence to suggest that these marks dampen Estrogen and androgen effects and can be passed on to male offspring. The female siblings of gay men can often be more fertile than other women, supporting this theory. So, being gay isn't unnatural or against evolution, explanations that attempt to depict homosexuality as a moral evil are not grounded in truth and are therefore damaging to liberty. The point I am making is that the biology argument doesn't hold weight in a modern society

---

kin and non-kin in Samoan fa'afafine. *Psychological Science, 21*(2), 292–297.

[44]Blanchard, R. (2018). Fraternal birth order, sibling sex ratio, and sexual orientation of men and women: New tests of the revised theory. *Frontiers in Psychology, 9*, 446.

anymore as modern technology is allowing for rapid investigation in this field of biology that is quickly undermining past misconceptions and is showing the evolutionary role of homosexuality. Many may say that it is unfair to critique trans-people on this issue by claiming that a man cannot be a woman but once again I am not saying that a trans person can't live the life of their preferred gender, as long as this is actually sincere. Studies have shown once again that this theory from traditionalist radical groups of "this isn't biologically correct" is flawed. A trans-person's brain is much more likely to be structurally similar to that of their identified gender than their biological gender.[45] Cisgender men typically have a

---

[45]Rice, W. R., Friberg, U., & Gavrilets, S. (2012). (Same as 41)

larger BTSc (Bed Nucleus of the Stria Terminalis) than cisgender women. Males who suffer from gender dysphoria, even prior to transitioning have a smaller BTSc than their male counterparts, which is often around the size of a cisgender female. In terms of White matter structure, there is usually an 88%-92% similarity between a trans person and their identified gender before transitioning.[46] The cortical thickness of trans people is often much closer to their identified gender than their biological gender. In terms of how the brain communicates between each of its sections, the brains of trans-people are far more likely to communicate in a

---

[46]Guillamon, A., Junque, C., & Gómez-Gil, E. (2016). A review of the status of brain structure research in transsexualism. *Archives of Sexual Behavior, 45*, 1615–1648.

similar fashion to their identified gender, meaning things like emotional responses and sexuality are often more in line with their identified gender.[47] The overall similarity in brain structure of a male turned trans-female with a cisgender female is between 70% and 90% depending on brain region, while this number drops to just 50% to 65% depending on the region of the brain when compared with biological sex.[48] Studies have found that trans-women

---

[47]Rametti, G., Carrillo, B., Gómez-Gil, E., Junque, C., Zubiaurre-Elorza, L., Segovia, S., ... & Guillamon, A. (2011). The microstructure of white matter in male to female transsexuals before cross-sex hormonal treatment: A DTI study. *Journal of Psychiatric Research, 45*(7), 949–954.

[48]Burke, S. M., & Anderson, A. K. (2014). Gender identity and the brain: A functional perspective. *Neuroscience and Biobehavioral Reviews, 40*, 1–13.

tend to have longer CAG genetic repeats in the AR gene which reduces testosterone sensitivity and may be vital to understanding how the brain becomes different from its actual biological sex in uterus development.[49] The point I am making is that once again, there is strong evidence supporting gender dysphoria in actual transgender people, and thus stopping them from living their lives in the way they want is clearly morally wrong, but we must ensure that we allow trans-people to maximise their liberty without effecting the liberty of the identified sex. This is why I oppose transgender females entering cisgender female sports, as they still maintain an unfair biological advantage. I think that an actual scan of a person's brain is

---

[49]Guillamon, A., Junque, C., & Gómez-Gil, E. (2016). (Same as citation 45)

required to make sure the diagnosis of gender dysphoria is correct before hormone treatment and sex changes should be made, but there is no reason we should deny trans-people the right to live as the sex they are psychologically. Transphobic people often point to statistics on trans-people which are not grounded in truth. There are many conspiracy theories on trans paedophilia and sexual abuse but there have been many studies that entirely debunk these claims and so they should be ignored. It is clear that gay people and trans-people are not biologically “wrong” or “immoral” instead they have been a part of human civilisation for centuries. However, this does raise an important question, why has the growth in transgender identifying people increased so rapidly? Human health is a key aspect of the Fourth Way. I think with the technology available to humanity today, we should try to do all we can to maximise human health which in turn will maximise human liberty. Humans cannot achieve full liberty during their lifetime if they are not healthy. There is some evidence linking the increase in transgenderism to the use of plastics in commerical shopping. Chemicals like BPA, BPS, Phthalates, Parabens and PFAS all come from plastics and manufactured human products. These types of chemicals are known as EDCs or Endocrine Disruption Chemicals as they create major hormonal issues and can severely damage the body over time. There is some evidence that these chemicals may have contributed to the steady rise in transgender identifying persons over many generations, as they started to be used in the 1960s and the rise began around 60 years ago.[50] The idea is that these hormone disrupting chemicals are affecting the growth process of the brain in the Uterus and creating an undeveloped gendered brain, leading to gender dysphoria after birth. These aren't the only problems these chemicals cause. They are linked heavily to cancer, dementia, decreased IQ, infertility and premature ageing.[51] As humans we must destroy these types of threats not only to human survival but

---

[50]Hare, L., Bernard, P., Sánchez, F. J., Baird, P. N., Vilain, E., Kennedy, T., & Harley, V. R. (2009). Androgen receptor repeat length polymorphism associated with male-to-female transsexualism. *Biological Psychiatry, 65*(1), 93–96.

[51]Gore, A. C., Chappell, V. A., Fenton, S. E., Flaws, J. A., Nadal, A., Prins, G. S., ... & Zoeller, R. T. (2015). EDC-2: The Endocrine Society's second scientific statement on endocrine-disrupting chemicals. *Endocrine Reviews, 36*(6), E1–E150.

also liberty. We must not filter our water to a level that is “commercially acceptable” we must filter it completely even if this means slight reductions in economic growth. We must remove these types of harmful chemicals from our food first, and over time through a gradual phaseout, our clothes and furniture. Unsafe pesticides must be taken off food and regulated more closely. Fast food needs closer regulations and corporations must be more closely checked to ensure their practices and products cannot damage human health. Overall, gay rights and trans rights are human rights, and we should allow these people to live as they please and as evolution intended them. Their circumstances are outside of their control and so they cannot be judged for making life choices that represent their actual biological or psychological makeup.

This next section will address the family as a part of society. The family is absolutely instrumental in ensuring social cohesion and making sure the spine of civilisation is kept intact. Parents instil within their children their shared moral civic values of the rest of the nation which keeps civilisation uniform and respectful of others. These values represent the civilisational spine and without these values, chaos would engulf even the greatest nations. Evolutionarily, these values existed to keep non-kin bound together in tribal structures. Humans have come a long way from tribal groups but we still follow the same animalistic tendencies as our ancestors, now just on a wider scale, as the best groups and shared civic morals were spread by dominant groups while weaker values died out. This is of course what the Fourth Way stresses at its core, an evolution by natural selection of people, states and ideas. The family and parents in particular are the keys to ensuring social cohesion in the long-term. Without proper parenting children do not learn key social cues or develop a realistic understanding of the world. Many parents over-compensate this belief by parenting to the extreme through helicopter-parenting. I have known friends who at the age of 15 and 16 were not allowed to use adult YouTube or go out with their friends unless it was a fixed social setting like a club. This type of parenting, though I understand appears positive, is actually extremely damaging. My favourite quote on this type of helicopter parenting is from the book "The Coddling of the American Mind" which explores this in great detail and goes as follows, "Prepare the child for the road and not the road for the child".[52] We should ensure our children have time to make mistakes, get hurt on the garden without supervision, play silly games and fall over as a result or fight with their siblings to make sure their brain grows awareness of reality. The brain is too complex to be passed down genetically in its whole, the structure of the brain is of course passed down, but the human genome is not complicated enough to be

---

[52]Lukianoff, G., & Haidt, J. (2018). *The coddling of the American mind: How good intentions and bad ideas are setting up a generation for failure*. Penguin Press.
52

able to code for billions of neurons. Instead, the brain aims to grow through experience and so sheltering your child from the adversities of life can be extremely damaging and could mean your child may not age properly and will be sensitive to outside challenges more than their other counterparts. Equally, parents are important in ensuring their children do well in life. I am not saying parents should let their children do what they please, instead they should guide their children through their life experiences, instead of aiming to control them or not caring at all. When that child has fallen over, the parent should act as a safety anchor of empathy and love and to explain to the child how what they did hurt them and that they maybe shouldn't do it again. The family is needed to ensure that healthy individuals grow up to become functioning members of society, and have respect for freedom of speech, property, critical thinking and other people as individuals. The West as of writing this is not doing a great job at this type of parenting. The Coddling of the American Mind discusses two types of parenting safetyism and "free range" by necessity. The middle classes in the West increasingly adopt safetyist approaches to parenting as they have more time for this approach than the lower classes who often adopt free range by necessity. Wealthier parents are often observant of their children's grades and will talk to them when they slip, they may encourage hobbies and be against extensive social interaction outside of school times, especially at a young age. Lower class parents often don't have time for this type of parenting due to workload and the stress of handling their own lives and so children are often left to fend for themselves. It is in these conditions that the most functioning members of society tend to grow as they are left to discover the world for themselves while the upper or middle-class children are coddled into their teenage years. This stark differences in maturity can be seen on university campuses versus apprenticeship post high school. Speaking from my own experiences, I will comment that reading The Coddling of the American Mind was like reading a description of my own classmates and peers in Sixth Form or friends from wealthier families than my own. The conclusion Lukianoff and Haidt came to was absolutely outstanding and accurate at least in my own experiences. You often find that sixth formers from wealthier backgrounds or middle-class families are much more childlike. They often become excited at small routine changes in lessons that wouldn't normally occur and tend to be enthusiastic about small outcomes whereas children from lower class backgrounds are often more grounded and behave in a calmer more collected manner. The contrast even in my own experiences is apparent beyond measure. We, as a society need to find a middle path, where children are free to learn but parents also care for their children's futures. The family is instrumental in providing functioning individuals that maximise their own liberty and therefore grow the advancement of society, and without these roles being properly fulfilled, great disparities can grow in civilisations which may hinder natural selection of ideas and the evolution of civilisation as a whole.

In terms of religion, I have very little to say on this matter. You are free to pursue any religion you choose, and the state should have no say on the matter. However, any attempts to employ religious laws as state law, force mass conversions or establish dominance over other religious groups should be met with brutal force. There cannot be a religious group that aims to dominate the rest of society as this will act as an illusion against truth and therefore hinder liberty. Discrimination of religious groups against other religious groups or people who choose to live a lifestyle they may not agree with should face the upmost severity of the law. There can be no tolerance at all of religious dogma, and I don't think the West is doing a particularly good job at monitoring the rapid growth of religious extremism. Fringe Islamic and Christian groups that argue for the establishment of religious law or forced conversions should face severe penalties for threatening the civilisational spine and these groups should be entirely outlawed, regardless of whether or not they have committed terrorist acts.

Immigration is another issue which must be addressed in this section. We must unpack the reality behind it before we move onward. Immigration without standards is not empathic, it is corrosive. We cannot allow ourselves to be wrapped up once again in our feelings when it comes to these sorts of issues. Equally, we cannot completely rule out immigration and have an entirely closed border. Societies that do not embrace differences of culture and opinion can never evolve and will remain stagnant. My proposal would be a points-based system of immigration to allow fairness, though I do believe that the system should be extremely rigorous and selective to allow migration into a country legally, which will benefit the nation. Cultures which do not come into contact with other ideas may maintain ideas which keep society weak. Through competition of ideas between cultures, a natural selection of ideas will occur, and by means of cultural osmosis, the best ideas will be absorbed into the native culture, replacing weaker ideas, while weak ideas will be rejected. By means of this process, the civilisational spine will grow more advanced and more able to withstand external challenges. Thus, migration can be amazing for a society.

In contrast, a society that allows to much change too quickly will find itself in a difficult position, the soul of what the nation once was may be forgotten or undermined. We must ensure that we allow small levels of migration to enhance competition in a civilisation and to reduce stagnation, but we cannot allow mass immigration which could damage social cohesion, especially from immigrants who may hold extremist views and could damage the liberty of others.

For the last section of this chapter, I will address the corrosion of liberty over time. I will address societal decline and slip in authoritarianism through the lens of the "Frog in the Water Hypothesis". This experiment aims to shows how cruelty, suffering and tyranny are allowed to become accepted by society through a process of slow manipulation. The experiment goes as follows:

1. If you put a frog in boiling water it will immediately jump out of the water through fear of death.
2. If you put the frog in lukewarm room temperature water, it will not jump out.
3. If you slowly increasing the boiling temperature of the water in time intervals the frog will remain put.
4. The frog will die without resistance or without knowing it is dying.

I believe this same process applies to society and its slip into tyranny. I think the process of tyranny is slow at first. It may start with a few months of brainwashing and alienation of the opposite political angle. Then it progresses into claiming the other side is a direct threat to safety and prosperity. After this an excuse is found to persecute the other group. Then the persecution begins slowly. After this stage, the government openly begins encouraging violence and an authoritarian regime is established. This must be opposed to preserve liberty and we must remain pro-active as a population and watch for tyranny. Those that do not have a respect for the truth and in particular, constitutional processes must be observed and opposed at every opportunity.

So, to conclude, society should be grounded in truth without ideological biases. Institutions should be adaptable and be centres of espousing the truth. Education should be rigorous and aim to enhance critical thinking and community. Crime is a plague that requires complex communal strategies to counter. We should be weary of polarisation and those who cannot think critically. We should recognise the slip into tyranny. We should ensure that the civilisational spine remains intact while also adapting to new external or internal threats.

FIGHT FOR YOUR
LIBERTY

On the Economy

"The first lesson of economics is that scarcity forces trade-offs. The first lesson of politics is that to ignore trade-offs is to engage in folly."
— Thomas Sowell, *Basic Economics: A Common Sense Guide to the Economy*

The economy is a living organism. Try to mess with its way of living and you will ruin the ecosystem.

There are several key things to understand about the economy before we continue in our analysis. The economy is a living organism and it functions entirely in equilibrium. I will pretty much outline immediately that government intervention in the economy is never necessary and never works. In fact, it often enhances the problem it tries to solve. Secondly, monopoly is not possible in a truly free market, unless it is government induced. Third, the banking system is essential for the survival of nations. Fourth, and most importantly, the economy is the allocation of scarce resources with various uses among a market.

There are not unlimited resources on our globe. The market uses prices to allocate scarce resources among consumers. If a price of a bottle of soda increases regardless of inflation, that is because the resources which have gone into making that product have increased in demand meaning they have alternate uses. This effectively means that the prices of consumer necessities and manufactured products are bidded on by consumers and the consumers decide how much they are willing to pay for those products and make a rational decision on the price. The beauty of a free market is that there will always be alternative items that can be bought to avoid costly items that a consumer may not consider worth its price. Instead of buying the stone cat litter which has increased in price, the consumer may opt to purchase the straw litter which is cheaper and does the same thing. This ignores the fact that there may be other brands of stone cat litter which can still produce the end product but cheaper and thus negate the effects of the rising prices. It is these types of companies that cut costs that succeed on the market, but we will address this later on under our discussions of economies of scales and monopolies. There is often much criticism from intellectuals about this process or at least attempts to regulate it to reduce prices. One of these strategies has been outright command control and another the cutting out of “middlemen” from business dealings. Let's assess the effects of the first one, command control. In the Soviet Union, Gosplan (the state economic planning commission) was responsible for regulating all prices within the economy. They controlled 24 million prices in total and only numbered a few thousand.[53] Economics Alec Nove estimated that if the prices of every product were estimated one by one every minute, it would have taken Gosplan 100 years to update its prices.[54] This naturally resulted in chronic shortages and rotting goods in warehouses. Food produced on farms was often left to rot in the Soviet Union in warehouses as it wasn't the main focus of the Gosplan for that week, instead they may be focusing on heavy industry like coal mining and steel

---

[53]Nove, A. (1992). *An economic history of the USSR, 1917–1991* (3rd ed.). Penguin Books.
[54]Nove, A. (1992). *An economic history of the USSR, 1917–1991* (3rd ed.). Penguin Books.

production. Another example of this can be seen in Venezuela in the 2010s when central price controls led to shortages of basically all needed household items. Inflation sky-rocketed to over a million percent by 2018 and the country is still in turmoil today.[55] This also doesn't even acknowledge the human cost of this inefficiency. Those thousands and in some cases hundreds of thousands of bureaucrats could be using their skills to do another job, while production and procurement prices between businesses actively determine prices of products through an automatic process of barter. What is the point in producing such economic inefficiency and consuming so

---

[55]Werner, A. (2018, July 23). IMF projects Venezuela inflation will hit 1,000,000 percent in 2018. *Reuters*.

much valuable skill and time in the labour market, when the economy can regulate itself through bidding on scarce resources with alternative uses. Marxists may argue this is to ensure equality, but to ensure complete equality you must attack other's liberty, and as Friedman rightly assess, a society which invests in freedom gets a great deal of equality and freedom whereas a society which invests solely in equality gets very little freedom and very little equality in practice.[56] An example of where this fallacy in logic can still be seen to this day is in New York. The city has imposed rent controls on its landlords basically for its entire modern history and the consequences of this on the city have been catastrophic.

---

[56]Friedman, M. (1962). *Capitalism and freedom*. University of Chicago Press.

There have been several major effects of this policy. One of these effects has been an outright decrease in the number of rental units available in the city. Between 2002 and 2014 the amount of low rent apartments in New York decreased by 441,500 equating to a 47% decrease in just over 10 years.[57] The total number of jobs in New York grew by 22% since 2010 but the total number of housing has only increased by 4%, showing the massive disparities in housing growth due to central

---

[57]DiNapoli, T. P., & Bleiwas, K. B. (2014, June). *The continued decline in affordable housing in New York City* (Report 3-2014). Office of the New York State Comptroller.

regulation.[58] This is just one example of government control making a mess of the economy, another common way of attempting to control the economy through central planning is price control. During state Capitalism in Lenin's Russia, the military secret police seized grain from the peasantry in the countryside to feed the workers. This was not efficient and only a third of required grain for survival was being provided by the state to the workers. The bread ration in St. Petersburg was just 50 grams per day. An extensive black market developed where peasant traders

---

[58]DiNapoli, T. P., & Bleiwas, K. B. (2014, June). *The continued decline in affordable housing in New York City* (Report 3-2014). Office of the New York State Comptroller.

would sell grain for market prices despite price controls on bread by government. The actual price of bread was 40 to 100 times above the price-controlled levels by June 1918. A less extreme historical example of price controls failing can be seen in Chile during the 70s. In 1970 the government introduced price controls on all consumer goods to try to curb inflation. The short term effects of this were positive, the weekly grocery shop was cheaper and consumer good could be bought for cheaper prices, but the shortcomings rapidly became apparent. As supermarket isles emptied due to the buying frenzy, there were shortages of goods due to imbalances in the economy. As we've already developed resources are scarce, not unlimited and so people bought more items as the price decreased due to price controls.

However, the actual rate of production had not changed which meant that shortages arose and because shortages arose, so did long-term prices as those resources were in increasingly higher demand. By August 1972, a basic basket of consumer goods rose by 120% in a singular month.[59] The effects of this nationally saw a decrease in food production of about 20% between 1971 and 1972 as it was no longer profitable for farmers to sell their produce.[60] In

---

[59]Central Intelligence Agency. (1973, August 31). *Allende's Chile: The widening supply-demand gap* (Intelligence Memorandum).
[60]Central Intelligence Agency. (1973, August 31). *Allende's Chile: The widening supply-demand gap* (Intelligence Memorandum).

addition, food imports in Chile rose by 149%, showing the increased dependence on global markets to try to fuel the government's overly ambitious price control policies.[61] Both of these examples show how government intervention in the form of price controls is never effective and always produces worse long-term outcomes than intended as it disrupts the equilibrium of the market. Now we will discuss what I mean by middlemen. There are layers to business production. Raw materials must be procured and refined. These refined product parts are then purchased and turned into final products. They are then

---

[61]Central Intelligence Agency. (1973, August 31). *Allende's Chile: The widening supply-demand gap* (Intelligence Memorandum).

distributed to retail and are bought by the consumer. There have been several attempts by intellectuals to change this process by means of removing or changing the distribution or retail aspects of manufacturing. There have been many critiques of retail stores by intellectuals who say that they are an unnecessary stage in production and are exploitative. An article in Times Magazine was published in 2022 which attempted to expose exploitative middlemen by listing that the top four meat processors in America control between 55% and 85% of their market showing their power and listing their practices as being exploitative for consumers.[62] Far from these numbers being a monopoly, their role is still absolutely needed. People like the convenience of being able to go to a grocery store and secure all their necessities in one place. It is only fair that for the maintenance of the building where that food is stored and for the wages of the people who keep the shelves stocked that you pay a tiny amount towards its running. The same case applies with the meat packing industry and other examples of middlemen. These companies provide convenience and save time for the average consumer who would have to travel to a butchers or farmers shop to

---

[62]Time Magazine. (2022). *Why this bipartisan group of senators has beef with the 'Big Meat' industry.*

secure the meat that couldn't be packaged properly in a supermarket, at least not in the amounts needed to be stored in inventory. Having a uniform system by which things can be procured adds structure and ease to the lives of consumer and means that food can be procured without hassle. Of course, middlemen are present in all sectors of the economy, but their benefits are still clear no matter where you look. In Tanzania between 1967 and 1980, the government attempted a collectivisation program to force its rural farmers onto collective farms. Private trading of farmed produce was banned and the government instead attempted to nationalise supply chains by purchasing crops at a fixed price from farmers and redistributing the crops to the cities themselves.[63] The consequences were disastrous. The farmers resorted to black markets and refused to sell their produce for the artificially low prices set by the state and middlemen re-emerged illegally as they were still an absolutely key aspect of logistics in the supply chain and so were needed as workers didn't want to abandon the convenience of their services. The traders would have travelled between towns and villages selling produce allowing for ease of convenience to the consumer. When the government announced that all trade had to be conducted through state run marketing boards, many didn't want to abandon the ease of buying from a middleman and so continued to utilise

---

[63]World Bank. (1977). *Tanzania: Basic economic report* (Report No. 1611-TA).

the services despite it being illegal.[64] So, we can so both attempts to regulate economic distribution of resources absolutely do not work and make things significantly worse in the long-term.

The next section of this chapter will cover the labour market and its unique issues. It is not a secret that trade unions hold huge amounts of power over business and many celebrate this level of influence as a protection of workers. There are countless problems with trade unions, primarily that they have no functioning role in an economy and so creates economic imbalances that effect national output. The phenomenon of

---

[64] Ayittey, G. B. N. (2019). *How socialism destroyed Africa. African Liberty.*

trade unions is also deeply fascinating, because they suffer from divine extinction. A trade union that gets too good at its job might inadvertently make hiring in their specialised sector of the economy too costly, thus reducing the number of employed in this sector and thus their own influence, as their memberships decreases. An example of this can be seen in 1970s Britain. So many people pour scorn on prime-minister Thatcher due to what happened to the coal mines in Britain in her premiership. The truth is however, that we shouldn't be blaming Thatcher, we should be blaming the trade unions and the Labour Party. The NUM (National Union of Mineworkers), were persistent in their demands for shorter work weeks, decreased working hours and increased wages. They also demanded that the government continue to fund inefficient mines that weren't productive to compete on a market level. The Labour governments throughout the 70s of course bended to these demands due to their Marxian tendencies and the 3-day work week became a reality. These policies caused the cost of coal to skyrocket throughout the UK as inefficiencies in the process of production raised costs. When Thatcher took power, it was clear that this economic model was no longer sustainable as it was a burden on consumers and on the state, so she did the only rational thing possible and scrapped the mines, thus destroying the MUN's influence entirely. This is a perfect example of how trade unions can destroy themselves. Their actions of greed sunk their sector into further unsustainable practices which burdened the whole economy. Power shortages were frequent throughout the 70s and the maintenance of the coal mines kept Britain energy backwards as other industries like natural gas and oil were hindered. Another example where this can be seen is discussed in Thomas Sowell's Basic Economics where he discusses the cost of firing public school teachers due to worker protection laws and trade union agreements.[65] He states that the price of firing a public-school teacher can reach up to 100,000 US dollars due to trade union intervention and work contracts, even if the teacher

---

[65]Sowell, T. (2015). *Basic economics: A common sense guide to the economy* (5th ed., pp. 257–259). Basic Books.
(Cost of firing public-sector workers due to union protections.)

was entirely not doing their job.[66] These types of examples of trade union power in the economy highlight their disastrous effects on individuals and efficiency in general. Attempts to increase working conditions of workers in different sectors of the economy have always backfired. For example, in the early 2000s the French Socialist government led by Prime-minister Lionel Jospin attempted to introduce a 35-hour work week, a decrease from the normal 39 hours.[67] The attempt of this reform was to allow

---

[66]Sowell, T. (2015). *Basic economics: A common sense guide to the economy* (5th ed., pp. 257–259). Basic Books.

[67] International Monetary Fund. (2004, May). *France's 35-hour workweek: Benefit or straitjacket? IMF Survey, 33*(9), 142–144.

the French workforce to be able to spend more time at home and have a better work-life ratio as well as an attempt to actually decrease unemployment by trying to make businesses take on more workers to make up for the lost 4 hours of work-time per week. However, this had massive consequences on the labour market that were not positive and achieved the opposite of the desired effects. Instead of improving workplace conditions, bosses tried to force their workers to be more productive making the workplace much more of an intense environment. The attempt to decrease unemployment through government black magic also failed as unemployment rose by 2%.[68] The reason this occurred is that the government calculations were misguided. Instead of hiring more employees for their businesses to make up for production loss due to time decrease, many bosses actually fired workers to try to save profit while making already existing workers take on more roles in the business to make up for the loss in manpower. This makes a lot of sense when thought about rationally. Why would a business hire more workers to make up for lost production time which would then cost the business another wage when it would be more profitable to fire some workers and allow the

---

[68]Investors.com. (2015). *France's 35-hour workweek doesn't work, top official says.*

company to shrink slightly into new targets, while forcing the hired workers to work even harder? This is the kind of logic that politicians are uniquely poor at, and the reason that economists are hated in mainstream politics because of their perceived "pessimism" which is actually just economic realism. Politicians have to champion themselves as protectors of the workers and their families, leading them to make decisions grounded in untruths that may sound popular to the masses but are actually damaging in the long term. This can come in the form of price controls for scarce resources, improved working conditions, cries to help the poor or taxing the rich, all of which can be damaging to the economy. In contrast, politicians that allow the economy to function in a natural manner often find themselves achieving economic success.

An international study of free markets in 2012 found that Hong Kong, a country with a Communist government had one of the freest economies on the planet.[69] From the 1960s onwards, the government announced a series of major economic liberalisation laws. GDP increased by 180 between 1961 and 1997.[70] Real wages rose by 50%

---

[69]Cato Institute. (2012). *Economic freedom of the world: 2012 annual report.*

[70]Census and Statistics Department. (1997). *Estimates of Gross Domestic Product, 1961 to 1997*. Government of the Hong Kong Special Administrative Region.

between 1961 and 1971.[71] These massive effects show that when the economy is allowed to compete within itself to discover its own possibilities, the lives of the populace increase as well. When the government attempts to act as arbiter to business on behalf of the people, the damage done is catastrophic.

The next section of the economy will discuss anti-trust laws and economies of scale. To address the latter, we must first explain what this means. Companies that reduce their business costs to a minimal level can keep more of their profits to invest in growth. When a company finds a more efficient way of

---

[71]Census and Statistics Department. (1971). *Hong Kong Annual Digest of Statistics, 1971 Edition.*

maintaining their business model at a cheaper rate than other businesses this gives them a major advantage. One of these comes in the form of economies of scale. Retailers can purchase huge amounts of product from a supplier at a lower price than a smaller business as they can bulk buy. One a retailer bulk buys, they are buying so much product, that the supplier can lower the price of product per head to razor thin margins as they are going to sell mass amounts of product anyway. This can then be replicated by the retailer in the form of lower shop prices. If the retailer can then find a way to reduce their business costs via means of hiring less employees or vertical integration of distribution layers of business, they can then cut their profit margins per head of product even lower. This is exactly what happened to super-markets in the US throughout the 20th century. Larger chains like Walmart gradually replaced local "Mom and Pop" stores. This was for multiple reasons. Firstly, Walmart and other big brands like Safeway often built their stores in places with easy access rather than in the middle of neighbourhoods. This meant distribution and deliveries to these stores were much easier and lowered costs as numerous trips were not needed to continuously re-stock inventory. Another aspect of these chains is that their stores were huge. They could keep massive amounts of inventory compared to neighbourhood stores like A and P. Despite having these huge stores, they also significantly reduced worker costs as they introduced inventory software which reduced the need for manual labour in backrooms. Their purchasing of warehouses in localities to fuel their stores also helped reduce labour costs as they got all their product from one source rather than multiple venders and the products came already ready for shelf display, reducing labour costs in supply sections of the business and in the actual store.[72] This meant these workers who would've been bogged down in this supply chain as it had worked previously could now enter other sectors of the economy and grow the economy by developing new skills. The classic politicians move in this sense would be to campaign on a platform of "saving local groceries" to try and win votes of these who are risking

---

[72]Sowell, T. (2015). *Basic economics: A common sense guide to the economy* (5th ed., pp. 104–107). Basic Books.
(On economies of scale in retail markets.)

unemployment due to the more effective business model, but as we will see, this creates inefficiency for the sake of votes. We can see how economies of scale are clearly useful to the consumer. They lower costs by cutting their own profit margins to razor thin levels on each product, operating on the business assumption that consumers will purchase large numbers of product while on their weekly shop. However, aside from the obvious benefits, the government of Western countries has persistently tried to reduce these economies of scale by claiming they are unfair. An example of this can be seen with the rise of Standard Oil in the United States. Standard Oil under the leadership of John Rockefeller introduced several reforms to the oil industry within its own business model that would allow it to thrive above competitors. They standardised oil barrels to make refinement and distribution easier as well as decreasing the cost of transportation on the railways through a similar process of bulk buying, but in this case, bulk distribution.[73] His standardisation of oil refinement made business all across the US much simpler as no matter which state you were in the measurements were the same. He also refused to waste oil that couldn't be used to combust, turning it into paraffin wax and candles. All of these actions significantly reduced the price of a standard barrel of oil from 30 cents per gallon in 1860 to just 5 cents per gallon by 1890, an 80% decrease.[74] The effects

---

[73]Chernow, R. (1998). *Titan: The life of John D. Rockefeller, Sr.* Random House.
[74]Chernow, R. (1998). *Titan: The life of John D. Rockefeller, Sr.* Random House.

of this decreased market price were profound. Oil became much more widely available and Standard Oil grew to encompass 90% of the market control.[75] However, the government did not like this success. Standard Oil was accused of maintaining a monopoly and an anti-trust suit was filed against them in 1906. Rockefeller was labelled a "robber baron" and his wealth was used against him as a sign of his power and influence. On a personal level, I think the contribution Rockefeller made to such an important part of the economy, well deserves him becoming a billionaire by taking a small amount of the profit of his business. The government was

---

[75]U.S. Department of Justice. (1911). *Standard Oil Co. of New Jersey v. United States*, 221 U.S. 1.

functioning under the assumption that a monopoly is maintainable, when in reality this isn't the truth. Economics is an ever-changing landscape and intellectuals often make the mistake of looking at economics through a linear lens, when they should look at economics through an evolutionary lens. You cannot take a snippet in time of economics and make assumption based off this time stamp because the truth is, the situation could look drastically different in less than a years' time. This is exactly what happened with Standard Oil. The company was found guilty of violating the 1890 Sherman Anti-Trust Act in 1911 and was ordered to break up its company into 34 independent firms.[76] However, just taking another look at Standard Oil's market share again by the time this court order was finalised, it had dropped to just 64%, which can hardly be considered a monopoly and was likely going to drop even further before the dissolution of the company.[77] So why did this happen? Well, it is a basic of economics that actively disproves the theory of monopolies. When a corporation grows to encompass much of the market share of its sector this creates economic inefficiency as there is

---

[76]U.S. Department of Justice. (1911). *Standard Oil Co. of New Jersey v. United States*, 221 U.S. 1.

[77]U.S. Department of Justice. (1911). *Standard Oil Co. of New Jersey v. United States*, 221 U.S. 1.

little competition to rival the company. This means that the particular sector of the economy may fail to grow as there is no competition. However, the monopoly will essentially destroy itself by means of divine extinction. If the company attempts to raise prices on its product due to its role as a monopoly (known as predatory pricing), customers may entirely stop using the services or products provided by the company and use something else. If we stick we the idea of Oil, users may move away from oil and begin utilising natural gas instead, causing the oil sector to lose profitability and goodwill from its customers. So predatory pricing is pretty much not possible for a monopoly. Now let's address the next idea that works against the idea of monopoly. Let's argue that a monopoly puts its prices up to a point where the consumer will still buy the product, but the profit margin is still higher than it needs to be. In this case, the profitability of the sector will cause investment from private investors into new start-ups in the sector which will attempt to undercut the prices of the monopoly which are raised artificially higher than they need to be. This will undercut the monopoly in the long-term and the new business with more accurate market value pricing will damage the monopoly's market share. Another aspect of a monopoly that creates inefficiency leading to its own death is creative stagnation. Monopolies often become inefficient as they have little competition and so their laziness induces lack of creativity and adaptability. This further enhances competition from start-ups who may try to make their own competitive business models which are innovative. Basically, this is the idea that monopolies are always vulnerable to innovation and as long as the government does not try to maintain a monopoly, its power is always shaky in the market.[78] Critics may argue that this model still doesn't work as a monopoly can just buy out competitors but let's look at that more seriously. A first idea to consider is that innovation moves much faster than capital. By the time a monopoly realises it has a serious competitor, it may be too late. An example of this can be seen in Amazon's attempt to buy Shopify which had already become too advanced by the

---

[78]Sowell, T. (2015). *Basic economics: A common sense guide to the economy* (5th ed., pp. 30–35). Basic Books.
(On monopoly myths and natural limits to monopoly power.)

time Amazon recognised them as a serious competitor.[79] Buying start-up firms may be cheap, but by the time a start-up has proven its business model, or innovation is going to make waves in the market, they may demand sky-high evaluations to be bought out or may be refused to be bought out at all for purely ideological reasons just like DuckDuckGo.[80] So, in short, measuring whether a business is a monopoly is nearly impossible and the businesses that do have a large market share are often

---

[79] Reuters. (2023, October 5). *DuckDuckGo CEO says Google's billions got in the way of a deal with Apple.*

[80]Harvard Business Review. (2022). *Why DuckDuckGo refused to be bought by a tech giant.*

only at the top for so long before collapsing from competition and their own mistakes.

Next, we will discuss the issues of the national economy on a wider scale. Firstly, banks play a major role in understanding the economy. Banks are instrumental for the allocation of capital and act as intermediaries between borrowers and savers. The same rules of supply and demand of scarce resources with alternative uses applies to banks on the national scale. When there is a high level of investment in the economy, interest rates increase to in response to the high investment demand while the monetary supply has remained largely unchanged. When demand for investment is low, interest rates lower, especially if the supply doesn't change.

This boosts market efficiency as when demand for monetary investment is too high, it may discourage borrows in the meantime, relieving pressure on the banks. When rates are too low, borrowers flock to banks to attempt to lock up the low interest rates on investment, meaning there is less pressure on borrowers financially and boosting investment in the national economy, helping the economy grow. Due to fractional reserve banking (when a bank keeps a small amount of savings invested into the bank by savers and uses the rest of the money to give to someone else as a loan), when bank runs occur and there is mass panic and attempts to withdraw money, the bank can collapse as it doesn't have the liquid cash on hand to give back to its savers. On the other hand, if a bank gives out money to borrowers on mass that may not be trustworthy (like having a low credit score) this can collapse the bank in the long run as it doesn't get a return on the monetary investment and cannot afford to pay back its savers. Both cases can destroy trust in the economy and causes people to save their money rather than spend it which can cause recession as there is a low money flow. It is therefore important that banks are allowed to maintain aspects of freedom in order to evaluate the trustworthiness of its potential borrowers while also ensuring that it cannot attempt to undercut other banks in reckless manner by lowering their own interest rates to levels so low that it can damage the stability of the economy. Interest rates must be competitive among banks, but they must also be realistic in order to ensure stability and transparency to savers and borrowers. Taxation is another key aspect of the wider national economy and is often abused by politicians to highlight some sort of cosmic justice. The government functions just like any other organism, it must have energy to survive and in this case, that energy comes in the form of taxation. The government borrows then energy of wider society to maintain the civilisational spine which is a fair and understandable trade-off. However, too much taxation can be greatly damaging to the economy and decrease productivity. If you increase taxes on any part of the business production chain, the end product will be more expensive, and the likely outcome is that less of the product will be produced because investments in these parts of the economies are less inviting as more profit is taxed away. For example, the oil windfall tax introduced in the United

States in 1980 saw domestic oil production fall between 3 and 6 percent because the incentive to invest in oil for higher profits was reduced.[81] The incentive for the end product will also be reduced to the consumer who is a rational thinker and who will assess the value of the product compared with its price. Both of these outcomes may result in lower levels of activity in a sector of the market due to increased taxes. If taxes are too high, the sector may die or become stagnant entirely as alternative products are found to satisfy the same needs of the consumer and monetary investment flows elsewhere. In addition,

---

[81]Congressional Research Service. (2006). *The crude oil windfall profit tax of the 1980s: Implications for current energy policy.*

when the government lowers taxes, the general populace has more money to spend freely or to invest elsewhere to match their own requirements and through assessing their own risks. This is much more efficient than thousands of bureaucrats assigning wealth to public services, and they cannot possibly know what is beneficial to millions of rational individuals. In the 1960s, the highest tax rate for top earners was 91%.[82] When Kennedy took power, he promised to reduce the top tax bracket to 70%.[83] Unfortunately, this wasn't passed until after his assassination but the effects on

---

[82]Internal Revenue Service. (1960). *Historical highest marginal income tax rates*.

[83]U.S. Congress. (1964). *Revenue Act of 1964*.

the US economy were very positive. GDP growth accelerated to 5% per year and as a result tax revenue grew as the economy grew.[84] The reason this occurred was due to a more dynamic allocation of scarce resources (money) in the market economy. The increase in disposable income of the general populace led to increased spending in the consumer market and investments in the stock market, as well as making it easier to start a business. In short, taxation is a poor form of wealth creation, I would go as far as to argue it is wealth destruction in the long term as it hinders the natural economy from functioning how it desires. Next, we will assess another issue of the national economy, that being

---

[84]Bureau of Economic Analysis. (1965). *U.S. GDP Growth by Year*.

the state pension in the modern day. In short, the state pension is not sustainable and needs to be scrapped or at the very least means tested for the bottom 20% poorest pensioners.[85] The state pension is inefficient because it is a promise that cannot be kept. The state simply cannot afford to pay hundreds of billions of pounds to pensioner who don't work for them to live comfortably. When the state pension was first truly implemented, the baby boom was occurring and so it was easy for the promise to be fulfilled as there was a significantly higher worker to pensioner ratio than there is today. The problem is that today, with declining birth rates, it is not

---

[85]The Guardian. (2024). *The flaws inherent in a triple lock on the bedrock of the welfare state.*

evolutionarily sound to keep this system in place which will grow more and more burdensome on the taxpayer as time continues. Though I believe on a personal level that having children, even in a gay relationship, is one of the most beautiful things a person can do in their lives, many do not want to pursue this path and we must respect their choice, but we cannot have it both ways. If you as a person are choosing not to have children, you cannot seriously then expect the state to bail you out in your old age and provide you with a pension on everyone else. This doesn't just apply to the childless either, if you have one or two kids, realistically this still isn't enough to maintain the social "safety net" we have established in modern times. Instead of supporting an unsustainable welfare state, we should instead provide individuals and families with their own money to pursue their own types of insurance. Annuity companies are amazingly efficient machines. They take monthly payments over a worker's life or a lump sum and use this money to invest in the economy to produce profit, which then is given to pensioners who bought the annuity to support them until they die. If they live longer than expected the annuity company is still responsible for paying them, if they die before their expected time, the annuity company keep the money left over.[86] The annuity companies invest in projects in the national economy like infrastructure, housing and corporate bonds. And so compared with the national state

---

[86]Investopedia. (2025). *How annuities work and why they matter*.

pension, we can see that these investments by annuity companies are much more desirable as they produce real world economic outcomes, rather than the state pension which grows ever more costly to the taxpayer and worker, and which doesn't produce real world investment. Lastly, we will observe government attempts to try and make companies more "democratic" and "fair" to its shareholders. In the UK, shareholders can call a meeting to remove the CEO and can even force hostile business takeovers that the board of directors would've otherwise opposed.[87] Though this may seem democratic and truly communal, the idea

---

[87]Financial Conduct Authority. (2023). *Shareholder voting rights and the UK corporate governance code.*

that everyone is involved in the company. This has resulted in consistently low rankings of market capitalisation for UK corporations in the top 30 category. Thomas Sowell details in Basic Economics how the Economist magazine stated that 13 of the top 30 companies were American, 6 were Japanese, 3 German and French and only one was British.[88] As of March 31st 2025, that number still hasn't increased with only 1 firm in the top 30 being British, showing the negative effects of these shareholders rights on the growth

---

[88]Sowell, T. (2015). *Basic economics: A common sense guide to the economy* (5th ed., p. 407). Basic Books.
(On UK corporate governance and market rankings.)

and coherence of a company.[89] Many shareholders simply don't have the time or care to be involved in their work in this way, meaning vocal and usually radical minorities gain control over billion-dollar companies. These people usually have no understanding of running a business or market fluctuations and so severely limit the company's growth, compared to control by a board of directors who are incredibly experienced in this aspect of economics. To an extent I understand why people are so critical of the bourgeoisie and the managerial classes. Humans nature is not positive and we do things with a motive. It makes sense that people will place these kinds of human

---

[89]Bloomberg. (2025, March 31). *Top 30 global corporations by market cap*.

expectations on people above them in business, but in doing so they are ignoring many aspects of human nature. A board of directors will act in their best interest yes, but their best interest is the survival of their company and the pleasing of their stakeholders. If they lower wages a ridiculous amount, first off the talent will flock to better paid areas of the economy that need their skills, crashing their business, but also the managerial directors can't risk strikes and a bad market reputation, thus they have to behave altruistically, even if what they are really doing is what will maximise profit. Suspicions of managers and authority will always be present as it is an aspect of human nature, but we cannot allow their valuable experience of running billion-dollar companies to be over-shadowed by average workers' suspicions. This brings me into my next point, the arguments against what CEO are paid to be removed. There are often stories from intellectuals in the news detailing how rich a CEO is compared to their average worker. First of all, this way of thinking is faulty because many of these men and women have worked their whole lives and taken risks no others would ever take to build their companies. They also have skillsets and knowledge that only tiny amounts of the population have from experience. This makes their knowledge extremely valuable due to its scarcity. Also, these types of arguments do not take into account the necessary measures for business survival. A CEO may own huge amounts of shares in their business, sometimes up to height of 50%. If the board of directors own the other 50% and feel that the leadership of the CEO is not helping the company and he should be removed, then the board of directors and stakeholders have to find enough money to effectively bribe the CEO to leave. This is why CEOs are given millions of pounds for leaving their positions which is often looked upon suspiciously by the intelligentsia. What they are failing to account for is that in business time is extremely valuable, and spending months trying to remove a CEO is not optimal. A large lump sum of money is sometimes the best way to direct the company in a new direction before chaos sets in due to bad leadership, which could lose the board of directors and other stakeholders billions of dollars. We will now re-address the issue of immigration through the lens of economics. Immigration can be very valuable if used properly, as we have already established from a social perspective, and economics is no different. Immigrants have brought so much economic advantage to the different economies of the world, primarily because the skillsets of different people change depending on their location. Polynesians will have immense skills when it comes to fishing, skills that other cultures will have never developed. Equally, a Polynesian will not have the same skillset of a German when it comes to vehicular mechanics. Both skills are of major use of course. There have been cases where the migration of different skillsets has enhanced the labour market in a particular nation. In the modern day United States for example, 24% of the STEM workplace is made up of immigrants, despite making up just 14%

of the population.[90] Indeed, according to the Harvard Business review, immigrants are 80% more likely to start businesses than native born Americans. In the UK, 30% of doctors are of non-UK origin.[91] My point here is that misconceptions about immigrants and minorities being "leeches" on the state are not founded in truth and actually the opposite is true. Immigrants are in search of better opportunities and have often come from environments of desperation and little opportunity, allowing them to appreciate the freedom and opportunities provided in the nation

---

[90] National Science Foundation. (2023). *Immigrants in STEM: Statistical report.*

[91]General Medical Council. (2024). *The state of medical education and practice in the UK.*

they have fled to, while the native populace may take these opportunities for granted. Niches also develop among immigrant and minority populations that may not develop in the native populations. Examples of this include the Jews in Poland, who due to their isolation and lack of rights, developed skills valuable in finances and ended up controlling three fifths of monetary activity in Poland by 1921. The issues of the national economy are issues that must be grounded in truth. The government must prioritise not what appears to be popular to the masses in the first instance, but instead what is best for the economy and populace over time. We can no longer allow politicians and their agendas to drive the evolution of the economy, we must allow the economy to thrive on its own terms.

As part of the last section of this chapter on Fourth Way stances on the economy, we will look at the international economy, primarily tariffs. The globalised market is an amazing thing, and we should do all we can to encourage free trade between nations (as long as standards are maintained for human health). Tariffs produce economic inefficiency and are a failure to recognise new realities. Globalised trade means that consumers can buy products from abroad which are cheaper than domestically produced products. The consumer then has more disposable income left to spend on other items which further grows the economy. In addition, free globalised trade boosts market efficiency, factories in China may be better suited to producing cars than factories in the United States. Whereas factories in the United States may be better suited to producing advanced machinery than factories in China. The international market allows countries which produce the highest quality items to be sold for the highest quality items of other countries. When tariffs are enforced to try and remove perceived “trade imbalances”, the economy very quickly downturns. After the Great Depression of October 1929, unemployment rose to a peak of 9% by December 1929.[92] Unemployment then began to fall with it reaching 6.3% by

[92]Bureau of Labor Statistics. (1929–1931). *Unemployment rates during the Great Depression.*

June 1930.[93] The unemployment rate never reached double digits contrary to popular belief of mass unemployment immediately after the crash. However, government intervention caused the unemployment rate to skyrocket into the 20% range. Under Herbert Hoover, the Smoot-Hawley tariffs were introduced to try and grow American industry and reduce imports. The tariffs were passed into law in June 1930 and within five months the unemployment rate had reversed and soared into double digits.[94] This would remain the reality of America for the rest of the 30s. In

---

[93]Bureau of Labor Statistics. (1930). *Employment and unemployment statistics*.

[94]Smoot-Hawley Tariff Act, Pub. L. No. 71-361, 46 Stat. 590 (1930).

contrast, in 1987, there was a stock market crash in the United States under the Reagan administration.[95] Reagan's response was simple. He did absolutely nothing, he allowed the economy to find its feet on its own terms. Intellectuals and the media criticised his administration for not getting involved in the recession to try to fix it, but the market rebounded by itself and had fully recovered by late 1988.[96] His actions of doing nothing also meant that the US

---

[95]Sowell, T. (2015). *Basic economics: A common sense guide to the economy* (5th ed., p. 57). Basic Books.
(On the 1987 stock market crash and Reagan's response.)
[96]Sowell, T. (2015). *Basic economics: A common sense guide to the economy* (5th ed., p. 57). Basic Books.

economy continued to grow despite a stock-market crash. Therefore, we can see that tariffs are illogical and damaging, and so is government intervention. The idea that trade imbalances can exist is also a logically flawed idea because trading consists of two consenting rational parties agreeing to a trade-off, thus the idea you can be unfairly treat on the international stage is flawed logical as the trade is mutually beneficial.

So, to conclude, we can see from my analysis with the help of intellectuals like Hayek, Friedman and primarily Sowell, that the less state intervention in the economy, the better. Reduced state intervention allows for the most efficient evolution of the market and innovate. Competition between business forces innovation which improve the lives of the population as a whole. Just as civilisations compete against other civilisations for survival, businesses compete against each other, and as a result business evolves and becomes more advanced which benefits the rest of humanity. Government intervention into this evolution slows the process by reducing competition and innovation and should be avoided at all costs.

I owe much of the credit for this chapter to Friedrich Hayek, Milton Friedman and primarily Thomas Sowell, three men who have contributed massively to Fourth Way economic thinking. Thomas Sowell's Basic Economics is a groundbreaking book for understanding economic thinking.

HARD WORK.
EVOLUTION.
NATION.

On Government

"The tree of liberty must be refreshed from time to time with the blood of patriots and tyrants."

— Thomas Jefferson, Letter to William Stephens Smith, 1787

The government should live to serve the civilisation. The government is in effect the soul of the civilisation.

As part of our last chapter, we will look through the nature and structure of government. This chapter will be short overall and will simply aim to explain how the government should be in accordance with Fourth Way political philosophy. The Fourth Way rejects tyranny and autocracy and is democratic. The Fourth Way believes in a separation of powers into a trifecta system. The Fourth Way also supports the codification of the Constitution as an anchor of the civilisational spine and to maintain order. The Fourth Way also supports aggressive federalisation.

Firstly, we will look at views towards democracy. Democracy in my opinion is one of the human ideas that has evolved over centuries and is the pinnacle of human thought. There hasn't been a single dictatorship in history that has lasted, and there will never be a single dictatorship that will last. Of course, I am not forgetting our historical analysis and so I recognise that all civilisations will fall into Caesarism at some point but ignoring this for a moment and simply analysing democracy versus autocracy as systems of governance shows that democracy will always be more effective. Allowing the people to choose a representative is a good way of producing coherence as it singles down the views of millions into an elite which run society on our behalf. Many people do not have the knowledge nor energy to have a persistent interest in politics for every political issue and even if direct democracy could work, it would produce nations that are sensitive to tyranny of the majority on most issues which could threaten social cohesion.

The representative elite can be removed and is sensitive to the popular will. This popular will is not just of the poor, but of businessman and women and minority groups. Intellectuals often see themselves as having greater worth to society than the average person and it is not hard to see why they may feel this way. A person who has always been told they are intelligent and has received a university education will no doubt feel more knowledgeable than the general populace. The problem with this is that intellectuals do not possess as much knowledge as they think they do, and their knowledge is actually specialised primarily in abstract thinking and the ability to twist real life scenarios into ideological or opinionated categories through critical reasoning. There have been many instances throughout history where the intellectuals have attempted to take control of society and impose their will upon it as they view themselves as the shepherds guiding the sheep. The prime example of this is the Soviet Union, where an abstract idea was applied to society and the destruction and death caused by this idea still haunts Eastern Europe to this day. The point I am making is that autocracy doesn't work. Having an educated nobility that runs society is never going to work because they are often out of touch with reality. However, democracy means that the entire knowledge of the whole population can be harvested to choose which ideas are the best and which are the worst, producing a civilisation that puts these ideas into practice in government. If the ideas of one party fail to produce positive outcomes while in power, the idea of another party can be tried and tested to see what truly works and from this bedrock idea more ideas can be applied to build an efficient society. This is the spiral of evolution as we have seen throughout this reflection. It appears to me that democracy is a near perfect political philosophy, though it does have flaws of course. One of these flaws comes in the form of emotive popular will, as we discussed earlier in this book. I will not go over this issue again, I will simply say that it is imperative that the media and societal institutions always espouse the truth and are centres of learning and investigation rather than partisanship. But what form of democracy is best? Well, it is my absolute opinion that republicanism is the best form of democracy. It balances out the opposing interests of many different groups to produce an electoral outcome which is balanced and truly fair. Some critics may argue that this goes against my own philosophy as if a party got the majority of votes, surely they should be in power not the opposing party, which won through republicanist systems. An example of this can be seen in the 2016 United States general election, where president elect Donald Trump did not win the popular vote but did win the electoral republican vote, thus becoming president. However, my response to this is that the truth is not so straightforward in this case as to assume that more votes for on candidate or party equates to leadership. You must look into why the republicanist model was developed in the first place. Its primary role was to ensure that the interests of the rural farmers who were less in number than the town urbanites had a fair say in politics. This is why smaller more rural states in the US general have a higher proportion of electoral college votes to their population compared with more urban states. By proposing the abandonment the electoral college, you are essentially saying that the place where you live, its unique issues, culture and way of life should be prepared to be overridden by the cities simply because you don't have the numbers to match their voting power. These huge urban blocs will have completely different interest and values to those in the countryside, and this can cause issues in governance. There is often much talk of making new States out of already existing states in the US, and for the most part I think these suggestions are silly. However, there is one case where I truly believe this is needed. New York. The state of New York is incredibly divided. In the south you have a sprawling metropolis with millions of inhabitants and in the north, the state is more rural and farming based. It is not a secret that in the United States, the democratic party is more sensitive to the urbanite vote which often hold more liberal values, whereas the rural vote is often more Conservative and locked up by the Republican party. This partisan difference means that in a state like New York, the urban based New Yorkers often outvote their upper-state rural neighbours and tend to elect governors who have the city of New Yorks best interest in mind, rather than the whole state. This has had major consequences for the state of New York in general, much of the water system in the upper state is still reliant in lead-based pipes with the upper state towns and cities still having lead pipes providing water to their homes. Around 40% of pipes in Syracuse are lead based posing a major health risk. This has occurred because the upper state has basically been abandoned by the urbanite governors who are more concerned with winning the huge voting power of the city of New York rather than focusing on the whole state. This is exactly why the republican model of democracy exists, to prevent situations like this which can threaten social cohesion and in the long term, with enough time, could cause civilisational collapse through civil war. The republican model ensures fair representation of the different interests in society by negating tyranny of the majority in favour of a more balanced system. Thus, the republican model does not defy truth as described in this political philosophy through sheer voting power, it properly assess the effects of what happens when groups are left marginalised by larger populations simply because they have more manpower. So, in short, we should aim to adapt a republican model of democracy to maximise liberty of all groups.

Voting systems are another key aspect of how politics functions and can decide the fate of a nation. I will first start by saying that I truly believe that the best system of election is the American system I discussed in the last section, but there are things I would change, particularly to do with how the votes are measured and applied. Firstly, I would of course maintain the House of Representatives and the districts, but we introduce proportional representation for elections to this body. If we say there are 2 districts of 5 seats each, and the Democrats win 40% of the vote,

Republicans 35% and Libertarians 25% then this district would be divided as 2 seats for the Dems, 2 for the GOP and 1 for the Libertarians (roughly). In terms of reform to the electoral college, I would introduce ranked voting similar to the Australian model for this process. All the first preference votes would be counted and if non reach 50% they would be recounted until one-party does, this party would then lock up the state while ensuring fairness. The next step would only occur if I was applying this situation to the US, I think the UK has more than enough representatives in parliament at 650, but in the US the House of Representatives needs to be expanded. I would add another 300 members to the house to ensure complete democratic representation. So, what would the states look like in the UK? The nation would have to be divided into federal states with different districts. I would aim to divide the nation into 16 states just like Germany that are not biased towards a particular political view and which respect culture and identity of the different aspects of our isles. I propose a distribution of 200 electoral votes in total distributed between these states. I think a commission to decide the borders of these states would be the best way to produce nonbiased state borders. In terms of the models of the states, they should have their own state legislatures and governorships. As much power as possible should be devolved to these states to allow them to pursue ideas that work. The rights of these states should be supported by the constitution. I would also make the third branch, the supreme court, much more influential. I would make their role much more dynamic.

There would be a total of 21 judges on the court to avoid groupthink. The judges would be solely responsible for upholding the constitutions of the isles and a president which is found to be behaving unconstitutionally would have to adhere to the ruling just like in the US constitution. A president that purposely delays or ignores the court's rulings would be subject to impeachment and it would be the duty of the House of Representatives and the Senate to remove the president.

I believe strongly in civic nationalism. The nation must have one shared language, legality and values. Integration of migrants into this model of nationalism must be based on loyalty to a shared project, not blood or race. Society must be based around honour from truth and corruption cannot be tolerated. There must be complete government openness and honesty to the people. All spending, potential government legislation and all backroom talks between cabinet as well as meetings between the leadership must be wrote down and published on a government forum for easy access. There must be no place for lies or dishonesty in government. There must be severe penalties for corruption, and government boards of a multi-partisan nature must be opened to investigate the spending and financial activities of all representatives.

The primary role of the government according to Fourth Way philosophy is to maintain the military and state security. There must be a secret service that aims to protect both internally and externally the state of the nation. The state should invest heavily in this secret service as a means to secure security and it should have its own military branch. This secret service should aim to protect sacred life from terrorism and crime and should never be used in a partisan manner. Any attempts to use the secret service in a partisan manner should result with life imprisonment. In addition, we must build the military to be as strong as possible to protect our civilisation. We should invest in long term defence projects and technology. In terms of policing, the state should maintain a well-equipped and trained police force that can protect its citizens, cuts to the police force and military should not be tolerated as these weaken the survivability of civilisation.

That concludes the government section. In short, I believe the best system of governance is the American federal model, with slightly more power for the states, a stronger judiciary, and reforms to the way voting is done in the US. The state should uphold the constitution and the military for the protection of individual rights and the civilisational as a whole. Corruption should not be tolerated in any capacity and there should be constant investigation into all public figures.

Final Thoughts

The Fourth Way aims to enhance individual liberty so that natural selection can take place on a civilisation scale. History is a spiral of evolution that is guided by providence and their universal rules. The best way to enhance this evolution is by means of letting society do what it needs to do, while making sure the civilisational spine is not destroyed. Evolution must take place within its own means. The responsibility of government and intellectuals is to maintain a framework by which this evolution can take place. Social institutions must aim to maintain truth and honour in society while the special care of two parents in the household allows individuals to flourish. All of these things interact with one-another to produce individuals who are rational and think in their own way. These individuals then pursue their own interests and goals in life. The more successful individuals push society forward with their successful ideas and creativity while the lifestyle and ideas of less successful individuals die as society becomes more advanced. This contributes to civilisational evolution and the spiral of history. The aim of this book has been to introduce Fourth Way Liberalism, an ideology grounded in truth, realism, honour and chivalry. It has also called for a complete re-evaluation of ideology and intellectual thinking based on whether ideas can be true or whether the logic behind them defies reality. I have aimed to show how ideas that are not grounded in truth can never work and that pursuits that are not grounded in truth can never maximise liberty and thus contribute to a backward regression of society.

In short, civilisations must adapt and evolve. The structure of civilisation must be maintained through the civilisational spine and shared civic values. Social institutions should aim to advance truth is a primary priority and to encourage critical thinking while the family acts as a mini civilisation of its own whose aim is to provide social cohesion. Individual choices enhance civilisation through freedom of pursuit. This freedom allows the spiral of history to evolve and become more advanced through civilisational change which is passed on to society as a whole.

Published by Colt L Kingham-Davies

First Edition, 2025

ISBN: 9798286310760

For inquiries or permissions, contact:
ColtLKD@outlook.com

Printed in the United Kingdom

Printed in Great Britain
by Amazon

63181300R00181